50 IMPRESSIVE KiDS AND THEIR AMAZiNG (AND TRUE!) STORiES

HEY THERE, come on in. This book is for you. Yes, you.

How many times have you heard an adult say, "Maybe when you're older"? Almost always, they're talking about doing the best stuff, right? Well guess what. These pages are packed—and I mean packed—with incredible, amazing, completely awesome, absolutely true stories about kids who didn't wait until they got older.

I mean, seriously, you're going to meet a sixteen-year-old who laid a smackdown on an entire nation (while his dad was out of town!). Then there's the fourteen-year-old super-blogger who turned her passion for fashion into a multimedia, multimillion-dollar empire, all by herself. We've got four-year-olds winning motocross races and fourteen-year-olds writing diaries and changing the world.

You know who else you're gonna find in this book? Soccer stars, Olympic gymnasts, musicians, inventors, and one seriously messed-up teen emperor. (And I'm not even talking about the one who named a whole town after his horse!) (Don't worry; he's in here, too!)

So forget about getting old. Let's go hang out with some kids who did what they wanted, when they wanted—and made history doing it!

Onward ho!

—Saundra

THEY DID WHAT?

50 IMPRESSIVE KIDS

AND THEIR AMAZING (AND TRUE!) STORIES

SAUNDRA MITCHELL

ILLUSTRATED BY CARA PETRUS

• Puffin Books •

PUFFIN BOOKS
An imprint of Penguin Random House LLC
375 Hudson Street
New York, New York 10014

First published in the United States of America by Puffin Books,
an imprint of Penguin Random House LLC, 2016

Text copyright © 2016 by Saundra Mitchell
Illustrations copyright © 2016 by Cara Petrus

LIBRARY OF CONGRESS CATALOGING-IN-PUBLICATION DATA
Names: Mitchell, Saundra, author. | Petrus, Cara, illustrator.
Title: 50 impressive kids and their amazing (and true!) stories / by
Saundra Mitchell ; illustrated by Cara Petrus.
Other titles: Fifty impressive kids and their amazing (and true!) stories
Description: New York, New York : Puffin Books, 2016. | Series:
They did what?
Identifiers: LCCN 2015034431| ISBN 9780147518132 (paperback) |
ISBN 9780698411005 (e-book)
Subjects: LCSH: Gifted children—Biography—Juvenile literature. |
Children—Biography—Juvenile literature. | BISAC:
JUVENILE NONFICTION /
Biography & Autobiography / General.
Classification: LCC CT107 .M58 2016 | DDC 305.9/089083—dc23
LC record available at http://lccn.loc.gov/2015034431

ISBN 978-0-14-751813-2

Printed in the United States of America

1 3 5 7 9 10 8 6 4 2

Text set in Bell MT

This book is for Nikki, Gwen, Addison, Winter, Jackson, Janie Beth, Jacob, Cassy, Vinny, Shannon, Erin, Caroline Fraissinet, Kate Espey, Sam Sandoval, Emma Wallace, and every single awesome kid in my life! —Saundra

To Olivia—every day you amaze me with your strength, bravery, and grace. —Cara

Contents

50 IMPRESSIVE KIDS AND THEIR AMAZING (AND TRUE!) STORIES

Stevie Wonder

Stevie Wonder

1950–

Most people wouldn't be considered a veteran of anything by the age of thirteen. Most people aren't musical legend Stevie Wonder.

Stevland Hardaway Judkins Morris was the third of six kids. Born six weeks premature, he lost his eyesight as an infant.

Stevie and his family lived in Saginaw, Michigan—a long way from the bright lights of New York City or Los Angeles, but actually really close to another major musical capital: Detroit.

Detroit loomed large in the rhythm-and-blues music scene. It was the home of Motown Records, the Motown sound, and the music that many people believe defined the twentieth century.

Stevie was musical from the very beginning. When he was still in diapers, he clamored to play instruments and loved to sing along with the choir at church. When he was four, Stevie's parents got divorced, and his mother moved the family to Detroit.

There, he started his journey as a musician in earnest. He learned to play the drums, the bass guitar, and the harmonica. He wrote some of his very first songs in elementary school, and took his music very seriously. Stevie and his friend John formed a band together. They would play on street corners, and sometimes they got invited to perform at parties.

Stevie got his big break when he was eleven years old. The Detroit community was tight, and people couldn't stop Stevie from performing. It just so happened that Lonnie Johnson, of the famous R&B group the Miracles, caught one of those performances. When Johnson heard Stevie sing an original song, his jaw dropped. This kid was amazing!

Right away, Johnson got Stevie an audition with Berry Gordy, the president of Motown Records. If Detroit was a musical kingdom, Berry Gordy was its king. He'd discovered some of the biggest musical acts of the time. And now, he had the incredible Stevland Hardaway Judkins Morris on his hands.

Well, the first thing Berry Gordy did was rename him Little Stevie Wonder. Then he assigned a producer to work with him, to develop his sound and his songs. Stevie learned to play the piano, and started honing his craft as a songwriter. He recorded a Ray Charles tribute album first. Then came *The Jazz Soul of Little Stevie.*

Motown promoted its artists with constant touring—together. So when Stevie was twelve, he joined his label mates on what they called the chitlin' circuit. They performed at all the major black clubs and theaters across the United States. (Segregation made them unwelcome at most other venues.) Stevie's performance of "Fingertips" was recorded live at the Regal Theater in Chicago.

It was a hit. A giant, massive hit. It reached number one on the Billboard Pop and R&B charts, the first song ever to do so. Now thirteen, Stevie was on the cusp of becoming a great superstar. Only one thing stood in his way: puberty. When his voice changed, Berry Gordy was convinced that Stevie was done as a performer.

Well, Stevie wasn't convinced, and he wasn't going to take anyone's word for it. Yes, his voice was changing. But he was still a songwriter—a really good one. While he transitioned from kid to teen, Stevie wrote the hit song "Tears of a Clown" for Smokey Robinson and the Miracles. For himself, he wrote "Uptight (Everything's Alright)," "A Place in the Sun," and he expertly covered Bob Dylan's folk anthem "Blowing in the Wind."

On the other side of his teens, Stevie emerged as a world-class musician and composer. Since his Little Stevie Wonder days, he's won an astounding twenty-five Grammy Awards and has inspired sixty years of song.

And it all started when he was a curious little kid in Michigan, singing in a street-corner band with his best friend!

Making History, Changing the World

In 1967, Susan E. Hinton did something remarkable. At the age of sixteen, she published *The Outsiders*. It was a novel about rival social groups in a small town, about how people could be killed for being different, and about how shockingly similar we all are.

That novel inspired generations—in the 1980s, it was made into a movie, and it remains an international bestseller to this day. And where is S. E. Hinton now? Still writing novels—and often tweeting about her favorite TV shows at @se4realhinton!

Param Jaggi

Param Jaggi

1994–

Do you think you could change the world? Param Jaggi does—and it's his goal to help other kids try.

Param has always been fascinated by science and concerned with our environment. In order to change the world, there has to be a world left to change. Riding in a car when he was twelve, Param noticed that the car in front of him was spilling out harmful gases. All the cars around him were. (Even his!) In fact, billions of motor vehicles on the planet were, all the time!

There had to be a way, Param thought, to turn that waste into something useful. So he started working on his first invention: an algae-powered filter for cars. Like all plants that use photosynthesis, algae love to eat carbon dioxide and excrete it as oxygen. Carbon dioxide is pretty bad for the environment; oxygen, naturally, is pretty good for it.

By creating a filter that screws onto the tailpipe of a car, Param introduced carbon dioxide to hungry, hungry algae. They eat it up and spit out clean oxygen. This elegant solution to a wide-ranging problem caught the world's attention. At the age of seventeen, Param submitted his filter for a patent, which is pending. And then he kept right on inventing.

Sometimes, Param uses his smarts to entertain himself. He invented a doorknob that uses his voice as the key. For the holiday season, he invented a device that synchs Christmas lights to music, creating a ten-second spectacular seasonal display every time he opened his front door. Science and technology can be both awesome and fun.

In fact, he uses that inspiration when he works on any invention. He thinks most companies produce things that are practical but not very awesome. His goal is to find the perfect intersection of both. In pursuit of that goal, one of his next green inventions was a watch that captures lost and wasted body heat and converts it into electricity for charging phones and devices.

Innovation requires an awesome idea and the passion to follow through on that. And Param understood better than anyone that kids have the best ideas. That's why, at eighteen, he started his own company, Ecoviate.

Ecoviate invites creative, innovative kids to share their ideas to change the world. When a really great idea comes along, Param's company then helps that kid create a **prototype** of the invention. Ecoviate offers the support and mentorship necessary to get that invention into the world. Even though Param has plenty of ideas on how to change the world, he wants to hear yours, too.

Param Jaggi believes that you can change the world. And he's probably right!

ACTIVIST KIDS!

It's not the adults who will have to contend with the environment in the future, it's the kids. And that's why Xiuhtezcatl (shu-TEZ-caht) Roske-Martinez has become an outspoken activist for cleaning up the environment.

The son of environmental activists, Xiuhtezcatl grew up surrounded by concerns for our environment. However, once he hit his early teens, he realized that he could start doing something to change things. He's a regular speaker at the Boulder, Colorado, city council. He convinced the town to stop using certain pesticides in public parks. He speaks out against fracking—using earth-shaking equipment to try to free natural gas and oil from the stone below.

As an ambassador for the environmental youth group Earth Guardians, Xiuhtezcatl encourages other young people to get involved. This group is composed of students, activists, speakers, artists, and musicians. They believe there are lots of ways to spread a pro-environmental message, and they encourage everyone to get creative with it. Xiuhtezcatl himself starred in a hip-hop video against fracking!

It's hard to sum up everything Earth Guardians is doing at once (for example, they have planted trees, traveled to Togo, Africa, to help conserve and purify water, and more.) They don't focus on just one area; there's a lot of environmental work to be done.

But Xiuhtezcatl thinks it's more than worth doing. He says, "This is about us saving the world for ourselves."

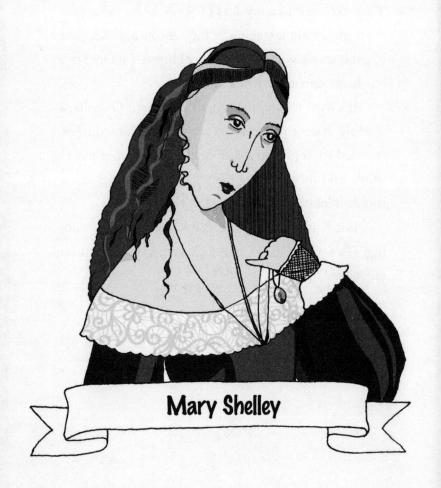

Mary Shelley

Mary Shelley
1797–1851

An unconventional girl in a very conventional time, Mary Shelley was a political troublemaker, consumed by ideas of liberation, free love, and art above all.

When she was only sixteen, her father sent her to live with a family friend. The reason for this is unclear. Some scholars think it was so Mary could get an extended education in her father's politics and philosophies. Still others believe that the quiet war that had been brewing between Mary and her stepmother sparked the move.

Perhaps the truth is a combination of both, with the added reality that Mary's father was quite impoverished and struggled to keep his family afloat. Pawning off his eldest daughter on a friend ensured that she had a home that he approved of, while relieving himself of the cost of raising her.

No matter what his reason, he couldn't have imagined what would happen next. While living in this foster home, Mary met the Romantic poet Percy Bysshe Shelley. They fell madly, stupidly in love—so of course there were a couple stumbling blocks in their path.

The first was that Percy was twenty-seven years old to Mary's seventeen. However, at that time, the age difference wouldn't have mattered too terribly much. The fact that Percy was deep in debt but anticipating a massive inheritance complicated matters. He kept promising Mary to help pay her father's bills; then he kept breaking those promises.

There was also the not-so-little matter of Percy's wife. That's right—he was married, and his wife was expecting a child. So not exactly the most ideal of circumstances for a romance to blossom.

But blossom it did. Mary and Percy met secretly at night, in a local graveyard. It was one of the few places they could risk being together without being seen. But soon, they stopped caring what other people thought. Without warning, Mary ran away with her much-older love, from England to Europe, where the pair traveled like **vagabonds**.

It was an artistic, literary life. But it was a hard

life; Percy's family still refused to give him any money, and much to Mary's shock, her own father disowned her. She didn't understand why. According to his very own beliefs, there was nothing wrong with taking a lover—even if he was already married!

It must have been a thrilling adventure—exciting and terrifying at the same time. Then, tired of being humiliated, perhaps, Percy's wife committed suicide. It was a huge scandal, one that left the couple constantly in danger of being homeless. No one much wanted anything to do with them after the suicide.

They eventually married, and they made themselves right at home with the notorious George Gordon, better known to you as Lord Byron, the famous English poet. In Byron's company, Mary and Percy spent a summer in Geneva, Switzerland.

It was a wet, miserable summer. Percy had disappeared several times to avoid debt collectors. And Mary, left alone to deal with the aftermath of their first child's death, plus the responsibility of caring for their second-born, had sunk into a depression.

In this dreary place, after such a dark few years, everyone's thoughts turned to ghost stories. Sitting up late at night, they shared German tales of the supernatural until Byron suggested that everyone write a ghost story.

The way Mary remembered it, she had terrible trouble coming up with an idea. It wasn't until a few nights later, after a discussion about electricity and the many ways people might use it, that a dread vision came to Mary.

Unable to sleep, she was tormented by a "pale student of unhallowed arts kneeling beside the thing he had put together." Walking the house at midnight, she slipped deeper and deeper into the idea. Intending only to write a short story, Mary Shelley penned the first few lines of what would become her most famous novel, *Frankenstein.*

Only nineteen years old, Mary summoned up the vision of a man and his monster which would continue to terrify and delight audiences for centuries to come. It was a stunning feat of science fiction—one of the earliest known stories of the kind. It pioneered a whole new genre, scientific horror, one that's remained popular ever since.

Generations of authors owe a debt to Mary Shelley, her unusual life, and her dark creation. And it all sprang from the feverish mind of a teenage girl, sparked to life by the invention of electricity.

Making History, Changing the World

In 2015, an American fourth grader named Sofia started a campaign to add women to United States currency. She wrote to then–President Obama asking him to put a woman on the twenty-dollar bill. She also included a list of women she thought might be good candidates. Since Sofia's letter, the U.S. Treasury Department announced that the ten-dollar bill is scheduled for an update in the year 2020. Plans are in the works to replace founding father Alexander Hamilton with an esteemed American woman to commemorate the 100th anniversary of women's suffrage. Looks like Sofia's dreams will soon become a reality!

Tony Hansberry II

Tony Hansberry II
1994–

Common middle school science fair projects: baking soda volcanoes, tornadoes in a jar, mints in soda explosions. Tony Hansberry II's? The most efficient use of a **laparoscopic** endostitch to close **hysterectomy** incisions. Whoa!

How did a fourteen-year-old Florida teen get interested in surgery techniques—let alone invent one? He was lucky enough to be selected as a student at the Darnell-Cookman School of Medical Arts, a magnet school for kids interested in medicine as a career. At Darnell-Cookman, medical classes are part of the curriculum. By eighth grade, Tony was already an expert at stitches—**suturing** was just part of his homework!

Tony's middle school had a partnership with a nearby surgery center. As a summer intern, Tony learned about laparoscopic surgery. With a medical mannequin, Tony used real equipment to perform practice surgeries.

It was a lot like a video game. The surgeon makes three incisions in a patient's (or mannequin's!) belly. These are called ports—through one, the surgeon inserts a bright light and a camera. Special surgical tools go into the other two, giving the doctor remote hands inside the patient. While watching the progress on a video screen, the surgeon carefully performs the surgery.

Surgeons had a special sewing machine they could operate laparoscopically, the endostitch. It was faster and gentler than hand-stitching. That meant that patients recovered much faster and had fewer complications. For some reason, though, they didn't use it to suture the incisions left after removing a woman's uterus. The question was, why not?

Using the medical mannequin, Tony experimented with the endostitch. Because of the shape of the wound in a hysterectomy, it was really hard to use the tool in the traditional way. The endostitch was designed to sew from side to side. After a few days of experimentation, Tony realized he could use it to sew from top to bottom. His method was three times faster and a lot gentler than traditional methods.

That meant the patient spent less time in surgery and healed more quickly afterward.

It was an amazing discovery. And an incredible science fair project. Tony submitted his discovery and won . . . second place. (It makes you wonder what won first place!) But, he was invited to a medical conference where he demonstrated his special stitch for board-certified surgeons. That's right. At fourteen years old, Tony Hansberry II taught surgeons three times his age how to use his technique.

The procedure is now called the Hansberry Stitch, immortalizing Tony in the field of medicine forever. It would have been a good stopping place for most people, but not Tony. He graduated from high school and went directly to Florida A&M University. At first, he majored in biomedical engineering—but then he switched gears to chemistry.

His next goal? Becoming a trauma surgeon. It seems like it would be a breeze, but Tony acknowledges that it will still take a lot of hard work and dedication. He told his school newspaper, "I don't know how I'm going to get there. I just know I will."

As the inventor of the Hansberry Stitch, he almost certainly will.

Pablo Picasso

Pablo Picasso
1881–1973

Pablo Picasso would become one of the world's most innovative, influential artists—but first, he had to learn to draw. No late bloomer, Pablo's first word was *'piz*. That's short for *lápiz*, which is Spanish for pencil. As the son of a painter and professor at a local art school, education came early for Pablo.

In those days, students learned by drawing figures from life models. Art teachers made their students copy the paintings of the masters, over and over. To become a master, one had to **emulate** them. As a traditional teacher in this school of art, Pablo's father insisted that this was how his son should learn, too.

Even doing copy work and re-creations, Pablo showed talent beyond his age of seven. He showed a great deal of dedication. Rather than studying his other subjects in school, Pablo neglected those to focus on art. When he painted over sketches, his lines were precise and bold. There was something alive in his work that both excited and frustrated his father.

In fact, when Pablo was thirteen, his father watched him as he created a painting of a bird, and then vowed to stop painting himself. His son had already surpassed him.

Because of this, the family moved to Barcelona. There, still just thirteen years old, Pablo took the entrance exam to the School of Fine Arts. Most students took at least a month to complete this exam, but not Pablo. He finished his in less than a week. Impressed, the school's jury invited him to take advanced courses. He was the youngest student ever.

Still, Pablo wasn't all that keen on studying. He wanted to create. Lacking discipline, Pablo often argued with his father about his schooling. Ultimately, however, Pablo agreed to attend the Royal Academy of San Fernando. This was the best art school in the entire country, and they were willing to take this sixteen-year-old prodigy as a student.

For the first time, Pablo was on his own. Better yet, he was on his own in Madrid, a sparkling, international city full of history and art. There, he could soak in work by such celebrated artists as Goya and El Greco. He made friends in Madrid and found much inspiration. But what he didn't do was go to class. Not long after his initial admission to the school, Pablo dropped out.

And then, he threw himself into art completely. On his first trip to Paris in 1900, Pablo decided to make the City of Light his home. He and a friend shared an apartment. They were both very poor; sometimes Pablo had to burn his artwork for warmth. Still, the city inspired him, and there, he met many of the artists who would surround him for the rest of his life.

At just twenty years of age, Pablo started to explore styles of his own. Thus began one of the most famous periods in Pablo's career—the Blue Period. Already, the first hints of what would become his **cubist** style were finding their way into his work. His mastery of true-to-life forms gave way to analyzing them, searching for the geometric shapes hidden inside.

Though he had no way of knowing it, Pablo was pioneering one of the next great eras in art history. For him, he was a starving artist, sometimes literally. Because he had no money, he lived on art and passion and inspiration alone.

Over the next seventy years, Pablo would earn worldwide fame. His politics and his passions inspired his work, and some of his most famous works capture the horrors of war. His gift and his long career made him one of the masters of modern art.

His work hangs in museums everywhere. He created some of the most recognizable paintings in the world. You've probably even seen some of it. Perhaps a sleeping woman in a red chair (*The Dream*) or a blue, angular man playing a guitar (*The Old Guitarist*). It's easy to pick out many of his pieces from the bright colors, bold lines, and imaginative shapes that make up the faces and bodies.

Working in nearly every medium imaginable, Pablo created more than eighteen hundred paintings, twenty-eight hundred ceramics, twelve hundred sculptures, and a stunning twelve thousand drawings in his lifetime. No wonder he asked for a pencil with his first words. He must have realized how much work he had ahead of him!

Angela Zhang

Angela Zhang
1995–

Here's the first thing you need to know about Angela Zhang. She invented a **nanoparticle** that's capable of outlining cancer tumors, delivering medicine directly to the cancerous cells, and avoiding damage to other, healthy cells. At the age of seventeen. While she was still in high school.

That's huge, right? A teenager invented a possible cure for cancer. Everyone's so impressed by that, though many people never ask how. How did a self-described science geek manage this feat?

When she was only seven years old, her dad asked her a question. "Why are manhole covers round?" Angela's original answer ("I don't know!") wasn't quite good enough. Her dad poked and prodded her, asking her about the other possible shapes. He encouraged her to think about why those shapes may have been considered but then rejected.

Though she didn't come up with the correct answer* at the time, she did learn something. It's really hard to look at a massive problem and just solve it. However, Angela realized that if she broke the big problem down into questions—into smaller parts—she might be able to solve those. Solve enough of the small problems and the key to the bigger issue becomes clear.

So how did Angela Zhang come up with her amazing nanoparticle? Like this:

At the age of fourteen, she really, really wanted to get her hands on some lab equipment for her own experiments. She was ready to stop theorizing and start testing. Of course, she was just a high school freshman at the time. Her school didn't have the equipment she needed, so she had to find another way.

Rather than waiting for college, or just wishing it would happen, she broke the problem down into smaller parts. Who has lab equipment? Universities. Who controls that equipment? The professors. Therefore, the best way to get into a lab herself would be to find a professor willing to mentor her (and let her work in their lab!).

She wrote to the heads of many university science departments to ask for access. Most of them blew her off. Of course they did; she was a fourteen-year-old kid who wanted to play with millions of dollars' worth of scientific equipment! But one professor at Stanford University found her proposal interesting. So he invited her to the lab—but first, he gave her a stack of journal articles three feet high.

It was her entrance test. She'd be allowed to use the lab only once she read and understood all the articles. Flipping through them, Angela realized she didn't even know what most of the words in the articles meant. Then she remembered her way of solving problems: break them down into smaller parts.

She looked up the words she didn't know and read the pages again—and again until she started to understand. A year later, she could finally read and understand all the articles.

Finally, she'd earned the right to work in the lab. Angela couldn't wait. She had family members stricken with cancer, so she had one big question: How do we cure it? Scientists and doctors have been working on this problem for decades—it's way too big a problem for one kid from California to solve in an afternoon.

Once more, Angela broke it down into smaller problems. How could doctors get a better image of which kind of cancer actually existed in a patient? How could they get medicine directly to those cells without harming healthy cells? Working on this problem for the next two years, Angela eventually came up with her metallic nanoparticle idea.

And what an idea it was. It was so groundbreaking, Angela won one hundred thousand dollars in a national science competition for her discovery. After that, she had her pick of universities—she chose Harvard. Angela's prodigy story could have ended there. No doubt she'll continue to be a vibrant and important part of biomedical research in the years to come.

But she knew that she'd had advantages other kids didn't. Her dad was a professor at a university, which gave her the idea to ask other professors for lab access. Her family supported her research; her mentor professor broadened her education. In short, there were lots of little steps that led to Angela's big discovery.

So along with classmates Jennifer Chen and Carl Gao, she explored the big problem: some kids didn't have the resources to experiment. So who does have the resources? How could they be shared?

By answering the smaller questions, Angela and her teammates solved the big problem. Trucks + used science equipment + science students from local universities equals Labs on Wheels. This idea was a finalist for a McKinley Family Grant. It's already under way and working to bring science to even more kids.

And that's how seventeen-year-old Angela Zhang came up with a possible cure for cancer in high school. It might be how you invent the next big thing, too. Start small and work your way up!

---

* Manhole covers are round for a couple of reasons. First, even if they're turned on their sides, they can't fall down into the hole like a square cover could. Second, you don't have to turn them a certain way to make them fit properly. No matter how you put a round cover on a round hole, it fits!

Alexander the Great

Alexander III
of Macedon

356–323 BC

Better known to you as Alexander the Great, Alexander III of Macedon grew up to be a seriously hardcore battle king. But first, he had to be a seriously hard-core battle prince.

In the art of war, his training started early. His trainer, Leonidas, didn't believe in the soft touch. Or even the medium-soft touch. In fact, it was all enforced marches, hours of drills, and oh yeah, very little food.

Though Alexander's mother tried to sneak him treats, Leonidas searched the prince's belongings. When he found sweets from the queen, he threw them all out. Then he made Alexander take another punishment run.

This was the way Macedonians raised young warriors—but it wasn't all physical training.

A young king in training had to learn **rhetoric**, logic, **oration**, and philosophy. It was important for him to be curious about mathematics, science, and diplomacy.

Since Alexander would one day rule a vast empire, he didn't get just any tutor. Nope. Alexander's first teacher was the philosopher Aristotle. Beat that for famous teachers! It turned out that Alexander was a bright student. He attended his lessons, then sought out more to learn.

Since he was the prince, he could pretty much go meet any famous person he wanted to. So Alexander decided to visit Diogenes. Diogenes was a great thinker, but pretty quirky. He was known for sleeping in one of the giant clay pots the Greeks used to store grain.

Diogenes was sitting in an open courtyard when Alexander dropped in for a chat. Brashly, Alexander asked him, "So what could somebody rich and famous like me do for you?" He loved it when Diogenes told him he could quit casting a shadow on him.

His friends weren't only the rich and famous kind. When Alexander was twelve, he tamed a wild horse on his own. As his father, King Philip of Macedon, looked on, Alexander took control of the warhorse that would be his steed for the rest of his life.

(For real, he loved that horse. He named it Bucephalus. Later, when he was doing all that conquering, he named a town after it.)

The conquering started pretty early, too. The king, Alexander's dad, had to go lay a smackdown on some invaders in Thrace. Did he appoint governors or councilmen to rule the empire in his absence? No. He left sixteen-year-old Alexander in charge.

Acting as king and commander in chief, Alexander took the position seriously. While the main Macedonian army was in Thrace with his dad, the Maedi tribe decided to take advantage. They figured Macedon was unprotected, what with only a kid defending it.

Sounds good in theory, but no. Alexander assembled his own army. Then he marched up to the Maedi and gave them the smackdown of a lifetime. This sixteen-year-old general drove the Maedi out of Macedon. Then he captured their capital city. Then he renamed it Alexandroupolis!

Alexander's dad was thrilled. He made Alexander one of his senior generals. Off Alexander went again, this time to invade Greece. Worried that all of Greece would attack when they realized what he was doing, Alexander pretended to be invading Illyria instead.

The Illyrians weren't thrilled with this **gambit** and fought back. Alexander handily whipped them, then together with his father invaded Greece. The Sacred Band of Thebes waited there for them—they were a special military force made up of 150 couples. The theory behind this battalion was that soldiers would fight even harder if their loved ones were at their side. It had worked in the past. The Sacred Band of Thebes was famous for turning the tide of war in their favor. They were, however, no match for an eighteen-year-old Alexander, whose troops slaughtered them all.

Alexander took the throne when he was twenty, after his father's assassination. From regent to king, Alexander now commanded the whole Macedonian army.

He went on to conquer Egypt, Persia, Asia . . . and pretty much anything else he wanted. By the time he reached his death at age thirty-two, Alexander commanded the largest empire the world had ever seen. He built more than seventy cities and named most of them after himself.

Except for Bucephala, of course. That was still named after his horse.

ACTIVIST KIDS!

After the end of World War II, nations around the world started to develop nuclear weapons programs at an alarming rate. The United States and the Soviet Union were particularly antagonistic to each other.

Over the next few decades, the leadership of both countries argued—all while creating a huge stockpile of nuclear weapons. People referred to this as the Cold War.

Frustrated by this continuing Cold War and worried about her own future, ten-year-old Samantha Smith wrote a letter to Soviet General Secretary Yuri Andropov. Much to her surprise, Andropov replied to her letter, and invited her to visit the Soviet Union. This trip made the ten-year-old into international news.

People proclaimed her a Goodwill Ambassador

between the United States and the Soviet Union. When Samantha returned from her visit, she wrote a book about her experiences. Her choice to write a letter, to talk out the problems between two countries, changed the world.

Mo'ne Davis

Mo'ne Davis
2001–

You can be forgiven for thinking that Mo'ne Davis is a baseball player.

After all, she did pitch her way through the 2014 season, winning the Little League World Series with her team, the Taney Dragons. She was named SportsKid of the Year by Sports Illustrated; she's the first female Little Leaguer ever to appear on the magazine's cover. Her wicked fastball was the talk of baseball during her pennant run.

Mo'ne fires her cannon-fast pitches with geometric precision. She may not be as physically strong as a male pitcher, but she understands the science behind the pitch. Time and time again, the speed gun clocks her pitches at more than seventy mph.

But Mo'ne David is not a baseball player.

Well, she is. But she was discovered while playing

football with her cousins. When she tosses the pigskin ball around, she does it with perfect spirals. She has an arm that quarterbacks would love to have—but she's not a football player, either. Mo'ne's first love and favorite sport is basketball.

That's right. This talented athlete has conquered the Little League World Series (she pitched a shutout—a whole game without giving up a run to any batter!), but her heart belongs to basketball. Only five feet four, Mo'ne manages to dominate the court with speed and accuracy.

Not to mention presence: as of this writing, Mo'ne is an eigth grader who plays for the *high school* basketball team. She doesn't just fill in—she's the captain. Which makes absolute sense, because in 2015, she signed with the internationally-famous basketball team, The Harlem Globetrotters. The minute she turns eighteen, she already has a pro basketball career waiting for her!

If she decides she wants to finish college first— she's said she wants to play ball for the University of Connecticut—she can probably write her own ticket. Schools would love to have Mo'ne as part of their program. In fact, University of Connecticut was so excited at the prospect of having her as a student, they broke recruiting rules to congratulate her on her World Series run.

In the meantime, Mo'ne hasn't given up on other sports. She and the Taney Dragons made it to the Little League World Series again. And, she says, she still likes to play a pickup game of just about anything. One thing is for sure. We're going to enjoy having Mo'ne Davis around for a good long while in American athletics!

Deborah Sampson

Deborah Sampson
1760–1827

Born in Colonial Massachusetts in 1760, Deborah Sampson is best known as the girl who disguised herself as a boy and fought in the American Revolutionary War.

Much like Mulan, Deborah borrowed a male relative's identity (in her case, that of her dead brother, Robert Shurtleff Sampson) to enlist in the military. During her service, she successfully hid her identity as a woman, even through several injuries. It wasn't until she was overcome by an infection from one of her wounds that her secret was discovered.

However, joining the army wasn't Deborah's initial goal. No—what she wanted was to see the world.

Due to her family's abject poverty, Deborah spent most of her teenage years as an indentured servant. That means that in exchange for a sum of money up front (probably used to pay her family's debts), Deborah agreed to work for a family for a set period of time. Most indentures lasted five to seven years. At the end of the contract, the servant was free to go and resume life as an ordinary citizen.

Jeremiah and Susannah Thomas owned Deborah's indenture. While Deborah was in their home to work as a maid, she also got an education. The Thomases were patriots—citizens who advocated for a United States free of British rule. Debate and political discussion often filled the Thomas home, firing Deborah's curiosity.

Soon, Deborah realized there was a lot more to the world than little Middleboro, Massachusetts. A bright girl, she wasn't satisfied with merely hearing other people talk about foreign affairs, and the state of this new Colonial union. She wanted to experience it. And because she lived in a time when women weren't supposed to explore without a chaperone, she realized there was only one thing she could do.

Get a chaperone? No way. She sewed herself men's clothing and disguised herself as a boy. It seemed like a good idea, but she wasn't entirely sure. She tried brief trips out in Middleboro to see if she could pass as a man. No problem, it seemed. Each time, she came and went, unnoticed.

Because she was fairly tall for a woman, she had no problem passing for a young man. When her indenture ended, Deborah found herself free to do anything she pleased. To support herself, she taught school, but she still longed for adventure.

Somehow, she found herself at the door of a local fortune-teller. She thought for sure, this was the best way to find out if she could get away with this masquerade in the long term. The fortune-teller took one look at Deborah in her disguise and had but one question: she believed this boy was destined to do uncommon things, so why hadn't he tried yet?

That settled it. Certain that she was onto something, Deborah bought a man's hat and shoes, and plotted her next step. Soon, she realized that the best way to travel far and wide (and get paid for it) would be to join the military. The American Revolutionary War was an honorable cause, and it offered Deborah the chance to experience the world.

In her handmade man's suit, Deborah presented herself as Robert Shurtleff Sampson, and was mustered into the army.

She was no slacker, either. She fought in the Battle of Tarrytown, among other skirmishes in New York. Wounded in battle repeatedly, Deborah managed to hide her true identity by caring for her own wounds. In one instance, she dug a musket ball out of her leg with a penknife. It took her longer to recover from these injuries, but at least her secret was safe.

When she was assigned to take care of another wounded soldier, she was shocked to discover that the civilian housing them was a Tory—a loyal British subject. Sadly, her patient died. But now Deborah had the intelligence she needed to capture a traitor to the Revolutionary cause. With the help of the family's daughter, Deborah led a raid on the house and captured fifteen men!

Eventually, her identity was exposed. But instead of being punished, she was celebrated. Her military service was both honorable and remarkable. Deborah won a pension for her time in the military; her husband was allowed to collect survivor's benefits when she passed away.

Though she's remembered as a Revolutionary War veteran, Deborah Sampson would probably prefer to be remembered as something else: a woman (and a man) destined to do uncommon things!

Making History, Changing the World

During wartimes, teens have always played their part. Some, like Alexander the Great (p. 36), were the generals. Others, like Deborah Sampson (p. 48), were soldiers. And during the two world wars, many were spies!

Lord Robert Baden-Powell formed the Girl Guides in 1909 (exported to America as the Girl Scouts by Juliette Gordon Low). The idea was to create a service group for young women, in the same model as the Boy Scouts.

As the first world war loomed, the UK spy agency MI5 realized that Girl Guides—who were supposed to do good works, be upstanding citizens, and be moral, honest, and dependable—would be perfect messengers. No one would suspect a fourteen-year-old girl in a scouting uniform, no matter where she went. So MI5 paid them as messengers.

Carrying classified documents from place to

place, the Girl Guide spies would deliver crucial information right under the noses of the enemy. MI5 trusted some of the girls so much that they taught them to memorize messages—that way they could travel into more dangerous territory without fear of getting caught!

During World War II, the Girl Guides took on expanded wartime roles. Many were still assigned to be messengers—but now some of them were encouraged to collect intelligence as well. They worked with resistance fighters throughout Europe. Once again, they used their unassuming appearance to achieve things no one else could: they helped liberate children from concentration camps and ghettos, as well.

The Girl Guides were an important part of the UK's war effort, but their acts of bravery and sacrifice remained a secret for decades. However, once the truth came to light in time for a centennial celebration, it turned out that the Girl Guides were still doing their part to protect their country. It was revealed that Dame Stella Rimington, the first female director of MI5, had been one of the wartime Girl Guide spies!

Kim Ung-yong

Kim Ung-yong
1963–

There are child prodigies, and then there are child prodigies. Kim Ung-yong was listed as the person with the highest IQ in the world in The Guinness Book of World Records*: 210, a number that's off the charts. But numbers don't tell the whole story.

When Kim was four months old, he could talk. Most babies that age are learning to hold their heads steady and starting to make sounds. By the age of two, Kim could read in four languages—German, Japanese, English, and his native Korean. Other two-year-olds? Working on potty training, and probably won't be reading for another couple of years at least.

What can three-year-olds do? Well, they can do puzzles with a couple of pieces and understand simple commands. Guess what Kim was doing. Studying physics at Hanyang University. Not only could he do a puzzle, he was literally working on puzzles like the space-time continuum and the origins of the universe.

So it probably won't surprise you that by eight, Kim had one of the coolest jobs in the world. Invited to the United States to further his education, he wasn't just going to attend a regular college. Nope. He studied astrophysics at NASA. While in the United States, he also earned a doctorate in physics at Colorado State University.

This prodigy to beat all prodigies remained with NASA until he was sixteen years old. At last, he was finally old enough to make some decisions about his own life. And here's the thing. As smart as Kim was, he was very lonely. After all, three-year-olds in college don't get to go to parties. (They don't even know what parties are!) Eight-year-olds at NASA don't get to have friends their own age.

Kim was homesick. He missed his mother. More than that, he was tired of being a prodigy. He said that to him, it felt like he was a monkey in a zoo. He wasn't a real person, he was just a novelty. So after spending his entire life immersed in physics, most of it in a foreign country, he returned home to South Korea.

Much to the media's disappointment, Kim had a big change in mind for himself. Instead of concerning himself with unraveling the universe, he wanted to work on problems right here on earth. Giving up physics, Kim chose a field of study that made him happy: civil engineering. What's more, he discovered that he would have to start all over again.

Sure, he had doctorates—but in South Korea, he hadn't technically graduated from grammar school, middle school, or high school. He needed those diplomas to follow his dreams. At the age of sixteen, Kim the child prodigy started over. And sixteen was exactly the right age to start going to high school. When he started university this time, he got to enjoy the experience.

Now that he's an adult, nobody keeps track of his achievements based on age. The media are still disappointed that the child prodigy didn't become a genius scientist, but Kim doesn't understand why they can't see what's really important about him. He teaches at Chungbuk University and studies **hydraulic systems**. He's reached a kind of success that most people only dream of achieving:

He's very, very happy with his life.

---

* He's also one of the last. The Guinness Book of World Records doesn't have a "Highest IQ" category anymore. They retired it in 1990, after deciding that the tests used to measure intelligence were flawed.

Q'orianka Kilcher

Q'orianka Kilcher

1990-

At the age of fourteen, Q'orianka (KorEE-ahn-kah) Kilcher became the face of Pocahontas in the major motion picture *The New World.* Beating out hundreds of other girls in auditions, Q'orianka starred alongside Christian Bale and Colin Farrell to bring to life the story of the Algonquian girl who introduced England to the people already inhabiting North America.

Acting since the age of two, Q'orianka already had several unnamed film appearances under her belt when she won the role of Pocahontas. Movie critics everywhere praised her performance in *The New World.* Q'orianka's depth and emotion impressed even jaded moviegoers. Though the film didn't earn a ton of money, it made up for that in awards.

Q'orianka won multiple best actress awards for her performance, including one from the National

Board of Review and the ALMA Awards. Though being an actor was always her dream, Q'orianka got a little more out of her sudden fame. She discovered that she could use her fame to raise awareness for **indigenous** rights. Herself half Quechua-Huachipaeri (the descendants of the Inca in Peru), Q'orianka has a deep, personal connection to the cause.

And she's not afraid to speak out about it. Over the years since filming *The New World*, Q'orianka has become an activist through organizations like Amnesty International and Amazon Watch. The youth ambassador for Amnesty International, she participated in a United Nations discussion about the dignity and development of indigenous people, both in Peru and all around the world.

She feels so passionately about her activism, that at one time she was even arrested for it! When she was twenty, Q'orianka chained herself to the fence of the White House to protest a visit from the Peruvian president, Alan García. Her mother poured a black substance meant to look like oil over her head, to help her get her message across.

García had allowed companies to drill for oil in the delicate Amazon rain forest. Indigenous people opposed this move to exploit this land. Not only did they advocate for a change in the policy, they also protested with civil disobedience for sixty-five days straight.

Q'orianka was inspired to do her part to help raise awareness in the United States for the plight of the indigenous people in Peru and the Amazon basin. Arrested for disturbing the peace, Q'orianka let the police lead her away proudly. The point, she believed, had been made.

Activism is a huge part of her life. She created her own organization, the On-Q Initiative. She brings together people in Hollywood with leaders, activists, advocates, and kids from all over the world. Her goal is to continue to encourage indigenous rights around the world, and to help save the environment at the same time.

This doesn't mean that Q'orianka has given up her dream to be an actor, though. Since her debut at the age of fourteen, she's starred in more than a dozen films and television programs. Recently, at the age of twenty, she was cast to play a role in a biography about inventor Nikola Tesla, in a film scheduled for release in 2017.

No doubt Q'orianka will continue to explore her talent for acting—and her passion for activism in the years to come!

Claudette Colvin

Claudette Colvin

1939–

Here's the thing. Today, it probably sounds like a little thing.

In 1955, Claudette Colvin, fifteen years old, refused to get out of her bus seat for a white woman. She was arrested and fined. It definitely sounds unfair—why should Claudette get up? What made that other woman so special? But so much has changed since Claudette's brave protest, it's sometimes hard to see just how brave it was.

It was illegal for the Montgomery bus driver to tell Claudette to move that day. All the other seats were taken, and Claudette knew the bus rules and her rights. But Claudette lived in a time when blacks and whites had separate everything. Water fountains. Schools. Buses. Movie theaters.

If Claudette wanted to buy a new pair of shoes,

she wasn't allowed to try them on. She had to trace her feet on a paper bag and take the outline to the store. If she got to the doctor first thing in the morning, she had to come back at the end of the day. White people wouldn't sit in the waiting room with her. She wasn't allowed to touch a white person. No black person was.

The day that the bus driver told Claudette to get out of her seat, she was preoccupied. A popular boy at her high school had been unjustly arrested. Everyone knew that this guy was innocent. The community was outraged. Despite their protests, this young man would be in jail until he turned twenty-one. Then the state would execute him for crimes he hadn't committed.

The case infuriated Claudette. Around her, she saw adults shrug and sigh, defeated. The whole government was set up against them. What could they possibly do?

Claudette was sure that letting injustice continue wasn't going to help. When that bus driver told her to get up, Claudette had a chance to make a choice.

Despite the fact that gangs of white people still participated in **lynchings**, even though the Ku Klux Klan stood ready with crosses to burn—even though other black people who had stood up for their rights had been firebombed and murdered . . . Claudette said, "It's my constitutional right to sit here as much as that lady. I paid my fare; it's my constitutional right." She would not yield.

Arrested, Claudette wasn't allowed to call home. Fortunately, her friends on the bus reported the arrest to her mother. Along with their church reverend, Mrs. Colvin went to bail Claudette out of jail. When they got home, they had to decide as a family what to do.

Most of the time, people simply paid the fine for protesting the seating on the buses. It was easier—it was safer. Claudette and her family knew that if she refused to plead guilty, her name would be in the newspaper. Her face, too. People all through Alabama would be able to recognize her. If they wanted to, they could find her and punish her for daring to stand up for herself.

Claudette's parents let her decide. And even though her father sat up all that night with a shotgun, just in case, even though people threatened Claudette, even though they called her "thing" and "whore," even though there was a very real chance that they would try to attack and kill her and her family—Claudette decided.

She'd paid her fare. It was her constitutional right to sit in that bus seat. It was even the bus company rule that she didn't have to give up her seat. Though it might mean she might die, Claudette would not back down.

When Claudette Colvin said no, it wasn't just about a bus seat. Her no resounded through the United States. No, she had constitutional rights. No, all African Americans had rights. No, she would not shrug and sigh and wonder what she could do about a system that discriminated against her.

It wasn't a little thing. It wasn't just a bus seat. It was a spark. Claudette's bravery encouraged others. She persuaded people to take the chance, to risk their lives for their liberty. And she took it all the way to the Supreme Court—and won.

Making History, Changing the World

During the American Civil Rights movement, many cities became home to protests and demands for equality. In Montgomery, Alabama, Claudette Colvin and Rosa Parks had been arrested for refusing to give up their seats on the bus—sparking the Montgomery Bus Boycott. Birmingham, Alabama, would become famous not just for Martin Luther King Jr.'s nonviolent protests, but for a march that forced the world to take notice.

That march was the Birmingham Children's Crusade of 1963. African American children came together for a long weekend of peaceful protest, March 2–5, 1963. They planned no civil disobedience. They would not deliberately break racist laws to bring attention to them. All they would do was walk. Walk from one side of the town to the other; walk across the bridge and make themselves visible. They would walk downtown and ask to speak to the mayor about segregation. That's all.

It was entirely legal for people to gather in peaceful protest. Legal, too, to walk around town and to cross the bridge. Definitely legal to talk to elected officials! But when black children started streaming out of their schools to join the march, the government panicked. The police started arresting children. Many of those kids got bailed out and rejoined the march only to be arrested again. Since that wasn't working—the local government tried desperately to think of a way to stop this peaceful march.

Eventually, they sprayed the kids with fire hoses. As if that wasn't enough, they set police dogs on them, too. The police chief, Bull Connor, thought this was a perfectly acceptable way to end the march. He was one of the few. It shocked people to see children treated this way. The kids hadn't done anything wrong. They were simply walking in their town! Didn't they have the right to do that?

The Children's Crusade didn't create new laws or change any old ones. However, all those kids were a part of raising awareness. It's easy to ignore injustice when it's hidden from the public. These young crusaders made sure that the watching world knew how Birmingham treated African American children. Their bravery helped feed the civil rights movement, pushing the United States forward toward equality.

Enrico Fermi

Enrico Fermi
1901–1954

Enrico Fermi was born in a very different time, but his discoveries in physics would come to define ours.

How different? Well, as an infant, his mother sent him to the Italian countryside. There, he was cared for by a wet nurse—a woman who was hired to nanny and breast-feed other people's children. He wasn't entirely without family there. His older brother Giulio also lived with this wet nurse. The brothers grew extremely close. They returned to Rome when Enrico was two and a half, and they were inseparable.

Enrico and Giulio loved playing with mechanical and electrical toys, together. They would build motors, sharing a passion for engineering. When Enrico was fourteen, he found himself suddenly, tragically alone. His brother had developed an abscess in his throat. When the doctors administered anesthesia for surgery, Giulio passed away, only fifteen years old.

Though still surrounded by his parents and his sister, Enrico was devastated. Giulio had been his best friend, playmate, and confidante since they were babies. Without him, Enrico withdrew into himself. He felt as if he could never get warm. Retreating, he would bury himself in piles of blankets with his books—going so far as to turn the pages with his tongue so he didn't have to unbundle.

Around this time, Enrico found a nine-hundred-page book called *Elementorum physicae mathematicae* (Elements of Physics and Mathematics). Though somewhat outdated, it nevertheless opened the world of physics to Enrico. He was fascinated by the study of astronomy, acoustics, mechanics—the way they all came together to explain our physical universe.

Inspired by *Elementorum*, Enrico started to experiment. He didn't see any reason why he couldn't figure out a way to measure magnetic fields. From his time playing with Giulio, Enrico found it easy to start building gyroscopes. (They were good for keeping someone, or something, stable and oriented. Gyroscopes are what make it possible for helicopters to hover smoothly.)

The physical sciences excited his mind. It wasn't enough to know there were forces at work in the universe. Enrico wanted to understand what those forces were. His curiosity—and his experiments—impressed his teachers. This boy seemed to be a scientific prodigy. The proof of it came when Enrico was invited to study physics at the University of Pisa, at just seventeen years old.

At twenty-one, he graduated with a doctorate in physics. Soon, he was not only teaching physics to other students, he was exploring the universe with his questions. So this little boy who was sent to the country to be raised by a wet nurse became the scientist who discovered **neutrinos**, nuclear chain reactions, and more. In his research, he discovered elements beyond the periodic table, and helped engineer nuclear technology.

And he never forgot he wasn't alone when he started this journey to science. Enrico named his only son Giulio.

Lydia Ko

Lydia Ko
1997–

In 1997, Tiger Woods was the youngest golfer ever to be ranked number one in the world. That same year, New Zealand golf prodigy Lydia Ko was born.

However, in 2015, Lydia smashed his record to bits. When she took the number one spot, she was only seventeen years old (four years younger than Tiger was when he ascended!). That's not the only record Lydia has obliterated, either. Born in Seoul, South Korea, and now calling New Zealand home, Lydia started golfing at the age of five.

Her mother taught her to play and soon realized that Lydia had a gift for the sport. Suddenly, Lydia had coaches and training time, competitions and competitors. Joining her first official golf club at the age of seven, Lydia played the New Zealand Amateur competition when she was only nine. At eleven, she won her first national title.

One title after another, Lydia burned up the golfing world with her amazing skill. By the time she was fourteen years old, she had earned her place as the number one amateur golfer in the world.

With thirty-five hours of training every week, Lydia has a very full schedule. She's still a full-time student at Pinehurst School in Auckland, and she has to work tours and competitions into her calendar, too. She works, she trains, she studies—it's a lot, but that's what it takes to be a champion.

And like other teens, she's interested in more than one thing. Her favorite pizza is a Hawaiian (pineapple and ham), and if you need a fellow mushroom and avocado hater, you've got a friend in Lydia! She loves to sing karaoke with her friends. Her go-to musician is Lady Gaga, and in her downtime, she swims, draws, and plays piano.

Golfing competitively is Lydia's career and her first love. There are still plenty of competitions to win and titles to earn, though. So it's a pretty good bet that there are older golfers right now who should be quaking in their spiked shoes. Lydia Ko came for Tiger Woods, and they're next!

ACTIVIST KIDS!

When Jazz Jennings was born in October of 2000, the doctors assigned her male. That's how everyone treated her until she was old enough to explain to her parents and the people around her: she was a girl, and she always had been.

Her parents allowed her to dress and style her hair in a way that made her feel comfortable. They talked to her doctors, and soon—when Jazz was just six years old—she started to talk publicly about her experience as a transgender person. Jazz is the youngest person to ever speak out about being transgender.

Now fifteen, she takes her role as an activist and spokeswoman seriously. She does speaking tours to share her experiences, and she's written two books about the same. Every day, she works hard to raise awareness for transgender people of all ages, promoting equality for all.

Sacagawea

Sacagawea

c. 1788–1812, or 1878, or 1896

Check any list of great Americans, and you'll find Sacagawea's name.

For European settlers in the United States, she was certainly a hero. At the age of sixteen, with her newborn son strapped to her back, Sacagawea acted as a guide and translator for explorers Lewis and Clark. She spoke Shoshone and Hidatsa; her husband, Toussaint Charbonneau, spoke Hidatsa, English, and French. This made it possible for the expedition to negotiate and communicate with the people they encountered along their way.

As the party traveled by river, one of the boats capsized. The men around her panicked, but Sacagawea took control. She collected her baby, then the expedition notes and papers, as well as supplies from the water. Without her, all of the research Lewis and Clark had conducted to that point would have been lost.

Even though the expedition would have failed without her, Lewis and Clark didn't pay Sacagawea for her help. They gave a token sum to her husband, but Sacagawea herself—nothing. A few years later, Clark adopted her children (including a newborn daughter) and raised them as his own.

And that's officially all the historical facts we know about Sacagawea.

Her legend is greater, of course. There is more geography named after her than any other woman in the United States. Because she was, indeed, a hero to the European settlers searching for the best path to the Pacific Ocean. Sacagawea is alternately claimed or disowned by various indigenous people.

So, time for a pop quiz. (Don't worry, you won't be graded!) In general, we believe that Sacagawea was born a Lemhi Shoshone. At the age of ten, either:

A) The Hidatsa attacked the Lemhi Shoshone, and took Sacagawea as a slave.

B) The Lemhi Shoshone and Hidatsa met to discuss a dispute. Sacagawea and a few other girls were offered to Hidatsa men as political brides.

C) The Shoshone attacked the Hidatsa and lost the battle. The Hidatsa adopted the surviving Shoshone and integrated them into their community.

D) Some of the above.

D is the only possible answer, because A, B, and C are all true, depending on the speaker.

Okay, but we know that Sacagawea married Toussaint Charbonneau at the age of fourteen, right? Not really.

A) Charbonneau won Sacagawea in a card game and decided to marry her and another Shoshone woman, because he thought **polygamy** was a-okay.

B) Charbonneau bought Sacagawea and another Shoshone woman and forced them to be his wives and servants.

C) A violent man, Charbonneau claimed ownership of Sacagawea, forced her into marriage, beat her often, and threatened to kill her if she ran away.

D) Some or all of the above.

Again, D is the only possible answer. Sacagawea was twelve. She didn't fall madly in love with Charbonneau and accept his loving proposal. She was treated as property, passed from one owner to another.

Charbonneau decided that part of his ownership included marital rights. It didn't matter if she wanted to be with him—or even if she liked him. Charbonneau owned her, and he decided her fate.

At least we know what happened to Sacagawea after the expedition, right?

Wrong. We know that Charbonneau got paid for his assistance and Sacagawea did not. We also know that Clark adopted Sacagawea's children and raised them with his wife. After that, it again depends on whom you ask.

A) Sacagawea stayed with Charbonneau, dying of typhus at Fort Turner, in 1812.

B) Sacagawea escaped Charbonneau and returned to the Hidatsa people. She lived with them until she was shot in a raid in 1896.

C) Sacagawea escaped Charbonneau and returned to the Lemhi Shoshone. She lived out the rest of her days in peace, dying among her family in 1878.

D) All or none of the above.

Again, D is the only real option here.

So what have we learned about Sacagawea? We know she was level-headed, because she saved the boat, her baby, and all the expedition papers when everyone else panicked. She had to have been pretty tough to go on such a difficult journey when she had just recently given birth. She was probably Lemhi Shoshone; she was definitely attached to a man named Charbonneau.

But why did she go on Lewis and Clark's expedition at all? What did she hope to gain? How did she feel about her accomplishments? What were her goals?

There's no multiple choice on this question; there's only one answer: we don't know. Sacagawea never had the chance to tell her story. Everything we know about her comes secondhand. Even though she's one of the most famous Native American women in United States history, she's very much a ghost. Many people claim her. Many people have stories about her, all equally valid.

Sacagawea, the human being, is a mystery. Sacagawea, the hero, is entirely up to interpretation.*

* Personally, I prefer the version in which Sacagawea realizes that if she helps Lewis and Clark, they will take her back into the heart of the Shoshone people. She wanted to go home and made that happen in any way she could. Once the expedition was over, she melted back into the land and lived out her life with her friends and family, finally reunited after her long absence. In my version, Sacagawea is her own hero!

Magnus Carlsen

Magnus Carlsen

1990–

Things that Magnus Carlsen liked when he was four years old: skiing, playing soccer, building with Lego bricks, and memorizing statistics about cities in Norway.

Things that Magnus Carlsen didn't like: chess.

That, he knew for sure. His father had pulled out his old chessboard to teach Magnus and his sisters how to play his favorite game. The sisters dutifully learned to play.

Magnus, however, was bored. He'd rather play cards with his family. Or Monopoly, as long as his sisters weren't allowed to form an alliance against him.

The story might end here—just another kid who doesn't like a particular game, oh well.

Except.

Magnus's father brought the chessboard out again, when Magnus was eight. Why not see if anything had changed in the last few years? And something had!

Suddenly, Magnus saw chess as a game full of strategy, puzzles, thought. Soon, he routinely beat his sisters—one of them quit playing completely.

After that reintroduction to chess, Magnus was captivated. He read books about chess; he played matches whenever he could. He even played games against himself.

Chess took over his brain completely. He loved the intricacies of the game, and well, he kind of hated school. Instead of doing homework, he played chess. Instead of going to sleep at night, he thought about chess.

In one year, Magnus progressed as a player so quickly that he started to beat his father at the game, too. This was no ordinary kid learning a new game.

He was a prodigy. Magnus started competing nationally and internationally, burning through the ranks to the top. People called him the Mozart of Chess!

Magnus sought out new competitors online, but he hated playing against a computer. Playing a machine felt soulless to him. In fact, once he said, "[Computer chess is] like playing someone who is extremely stupid but who beats you anyway."

The real challenge was the masters and grandmasters of chess. The wizards who had fought their way to the tops of the international rankings, like Garry Kasparov, Anatoly Karpov, and Viswanathan Anand.

Immersing himself completely, Carlsen fell in love with the poetry of chess. The art and grace of it. Figuring out how to beat someone was good, but executing a brand-new move or combination was even better. He threw himself headlong into play.

By the time he turned thirteen, he had become a grandmaster—the second youngest in history. (As of this writing, he is the third youngest.) Ranked the number one player in the world, Magnus has the highest peak rating ever.

What he doesn't have is an ordinary backstory. Magnus didn't finish high school; he's not remotely interested in going to college. In fact, he rents a basement apartment from his parents (in spite of the millions of dollars he's made in tournament purses and endorsements).

In his free time, he's probably playing video

games with his friends. You might find him skiing. Some nights, you'll even catch him with the karaoke microphone as he and his family take turns at Sing-Song.

But you're most likely to find Magnus at a chessboard (or two or three). The game that consumes his life was a game he didn't even enjoy the first time he played it. Magnus Carlsen is proof that people may choose their own destiny, but sometimes, destiny chooses them.

ACTIVIST KIDS!

Jonas Corona's mother, Renee, started taking him to volunteer at a Long Beach, California, homeless shelter when he was just four. As he helped serve food to those who needed it, Jonas noticed that it wasn't just adults in line.

He saw children without enough food, without clothes, without places to live.

So when he was just six, Jonas founded Love in the Mirror, a nonprofit organization that runs food drives, raises money, picks up donations, and spreads awareness about the homelessness situation in Long Beach.

Jonas himself does many speaking engagements. He talks about his experiences and the people he's met through Love in the Mirror. The most important thing for him is that everyone has enough—that kids (and adults) can escape homelessness.

He named his foundation after his personal philosophy: "Everyone should look in a mirror and love what they see."

Emma Watson

Emma Watson

1990–

In an interview with Tavi Gevinson (p. 206), Emma Watson said, "Every article that's published about me has some reference to Hogwarts or Hermione or magic . . . if I were to do anything else, I think I would have to create another kind of identity for myself."

Emma is definitely best known for her breakout role as the smart and strong Hermione Granger in the Harry Potter films. But that's not all she's known for! Bright, ambitious, and driven, Emma has created a life for herself that includes fame but doesn't revolve around it.

Originally, Emma auditioned for the movie series for fun. Casting agents came to her school, and so she popped down to the gym to try out. She'd already been in a couple of school plays, so why not?

Ultimately, it took Emma eight auditions to win

the part of Hermione. The Harry Potter movies, based on the books by J. K. Rowling, were going to be huge no matter who they cast. But of all the original auditions, Rowling felt that Emma captured her character the best on the very first try.

That means at the age of nine, Emma started a full-time career as an actress. She took her work seriously. Memorizing all of her own lines, Emma learned everyone else's, as well. She often had to be reminded not to mouth the other actors' lines along with them!

For the third film, the director asked each of the movie's three stars to write an essay about the character he or she played. Daniel Radcliffe as Harry wrote one page. Rupert Grint as Ron never turned his in. Emma, true to herself and Hermione, wrote sixteen pages on the subject.

Always studious, Emma kept up with her schooling while working on the films. The entire cast had on-set tutors, but Emma wanted to excel. To further that goal, she learned to speak French, Italian, and German.

She aced the tests that British students take for technical and university placement. Her costar Daniel Radcliffe did well; he earned three AS levels.* But

Emma? She overachieved with four: in history of art, art, geography, and English language.

No one was surprised when Emma decided to go to college. Accepted to Cambridge, Brown, and Columbia, she attended Brown University in the United States. She said it felt like a family to her. It was a place where she could be herself for several years, instead of being the superstar she was to the rest of the world.

Attending college full time, Emma nonetheless managed to maintain her crazy schedule as an actress simultaneously. She filmed movies, took press tours, attended awards shows and premieres, and still kept up her studies. In fact, she told producers that she wouldn't sign a contract for the last two films if they didn't include time for her schooling. (Fortunately, they did!)

Since shooting the last Harry Potter film, Emma has managed to do quite a lot of things without resorting to a pseudonym.

Named a UN Women's Goodwill Ambassador, Emma speaks out on a variety of issues facing women in the world today. Because she's ready to move the discussion forward, she points out that discrimination against girls also hurts boys.

She launched the HeForShe Campaign in 2014. Calling it an invitation to boys to join the discussion, she said, "Both men and women should feel free to be sensitive. Both men and women should feel free to be strong."

As Emma continues her career as an activist, she also continues her work as an artist. As one of the most recognizable and bankable movie stars today, she uses her power to make movies that otherwise might not get a chance. One of those was the film adaptation of Stephen Chbosky's young adult novel, *The Perks of Being a Wallflower.*

For more than twelve years, that film struggled to gain traction. Hollywood wasn't interested in a story about confused young men and women who were just trying to figure out their own lives. Even though it already had a partial cast and a director at the helm, it took Emma to pitch the project to executives to actually get it made.

Emma Watson auditioned for the role of a lifetime for fun. She has since become an ambitious student, activist, ambassador, and artist—all before the age of twenty-five.

* In many parts of the world, including the United Kingdom, students don't work toward a high school diploma or take the SATs. Instead, if they're planning on going to college, they take tests called the General Certificate of Education (GCEs.) These courses are divided over two years—in the first year, you earn your AS level certificate; in the second, your A2.

K'inich Janaab' Pakal

K'inich Janaab' Pakal
603–683

Twelve years old was the age of maturity for the Maya people of South America. In what would become the modern-day Mexican state of Chiapas, one tween king took the throne and steered his empire to prosperity.

K'inich Janaab' Pakal ascended to the Palenque empire's throne at the age of twelve. Technically, he had become king three years earlier, when his father died after a devastating military loss. What was interesting was that his father was not the king. He was only a lord; the throne passed through his mother, who was queen. This made K'inich's claim to the throne very controversial among the other noble families.

The fact that he was only nine years old didn't help much. Since K'inich couldn't yet be expected to rule, his mother stepped in as the regent. It would be only a few years until K'inich reached maturity. During that time, he learned as much as he could about governing. He had a big job ahead of him, and he needed to be prepared.

One of the things he learned was that it would be important for him to bolster his claim to the throne. He had to remind people of his history and lineage. And he would have to achieve great things to prove that the gods approved of his rule. On a more practical note, the Palenque people had suffered many losses in recent decades. They needed a ruler to provide stability and to promote prosperity.

When the crown passed to K'inich, Palenque was still a fairly small town. Almost at once, K'inich got to work. First, there were the monuments that celebrated the glory of the Palenque's history. Not to mention the monuments that linked his own heritage straight back to the gods. (All over the world, a direct link back to the almighty was proof that a king was meant to rule. The Egyptian pharaohs did it, the Roman emperors did it—even English monarchs believed they ruled by divine right.)

However, K'inich knew that monuments alone wouldn't build his empire. He expanded the city bit by bit. He no doubt practiced diplomacy, because Palenque's wealth grew under his reign. However, the records for K'inich's deeds are sparse. Most of what we know about him, we know because of the temples and monuments he built to secure the throne.

From that perspective, his greatest achievement was the Temple of the Inscriptions, where he was buried. It remained sealed until the modern day. When archaeologists discovered it, they found a treasure trove of Maya history. The walls were covered with murals, tracing and retracing the Palenque past. K'inich's tomb remained intact—quite a find.

On the cover of his sarcophagus, archaeologists found the first complete explanation of the Maya universe. Before scientific exploration allowed human beings to understand the cosmos, in fact, every culture had its own beliefs and understandings.

For the first time, modern humans could get a glimpse inside the Maya mind—and it was all thanks to K'inich Janaab' Pakal, ruler at age twelve.

Malala Yousafzai

Malala Yousafzai

1997–

Winner of the Nobel Peace Prize, and a leading activist for a girl's right to an education, Malala Yousafzai had planned to become a doctor.

A good student and eager to learn, Malala enjoyed her classes. She and her siblings attended Khushal Public School in Swat Valley, Pakistan, with all the other kids in town. Their day was pretty much just like any school day: lessons, homework, recess. The buses were a little different—benches in the back of pickup trucks, with a canopy overhead—but like any school, there were teachers, friends, textbooks, and blackboards.

It would have remained that way if the Taliban hadn't stepped in. An extremist political party, the Taliban have very strict ideas about what people can and cannot do. When it comes to girls, they're especially hardcore.

They feel that all girls should wear a full-body **burqa**, a hood and gown that covers the body from head to toe. They don't think girls should be allowed to drive, or to walk outside without a father or brother to escort them. And they're violently opposed to girls getting an education.

As the Taliban slowly took control of Swat, Malala's hometown, they pushed more and more girls out of school. They demanded that all girls stop attending classes. No more television for girls, no more shopping or spending time in public. These weren't just gentle suggestions. They were demands. The Taliban would murder police officers and hang their bodies as a reminder of their power. They expected everyone to meekly obey their commands.

They didn't know Malala.

Not only did she insist on continuing her classes, she spoke out about the value of an education. She spoke to the press in Peshawar about her right to an education. Malala stood behind her school and refused to back down. Though the death threats started to roll in, Malala persisted. She wanted to be a doctor, and she couldn't do that unless she was allowed to continue her schooling.

The situation got worse. The Taliban cracked down. In a very short period of time, the Taliban had bombed more than five hundred schools, and they weren't about to stop any time soon. To get the word out, a student at Khushal Public School named Aisha had volunteered to write a blog about her experiences. Her story was to be published by the British Broadcasting Company, pointing a spotlight at the unfolding disaster in her community.

At the last minute, Aisha changed her mind. The Taliban shot **dissenters**. There was a very real chance that she and her family could be murdered if she spoke out. With Aisha's withdrawal, the BBC had to find someone willing to take the risk. If the world didn't know what the Taliban was doing, they could get away with anything.

Eleven-year-old Malala Yousafzai volunteered. She was four years younger than Aisha, but she took to the blog with fierce dedication. Chronicling her days in Swat as the Taliban tried to force the schools to close, Malala sent regular entries to the BBC for publication. Though she wrote anonymously, it wasn't hard to match up the blogger's details with the real girl's experiences.

More death threats came. Out of seven hundred students, only seventy continued their education. The rest rightfully feared for their lives and didn't want to take the risk. Malala continued her bold activism. Not only did she write the blog, she spoke out in public. One morning, she woke up to the sound of gunfire in her city. Her BBC blog had been republished in the local newspapers. The Taliban were incensed.

The outcry was so great, the Taliban had to back down—a little. They reluctantly agreed to let girls attend school but only if they wore burqas. This peace offering, however, was a distraction. At the same time they offered this concession, they sought out Malala Yousafzai. To them, the problem would be easy to solve. If Malala couldn't speak out, then she wouldn't draw any more attention to their regime.

Tracking her down, the Taliban waited for Malala to get on the bus at the end of her school day. She and a few of her friends decided to ride the bus a little longer. Instead of getting off at their regular stop, they stayed on board with the little kids. It was an extra ride, and extra time to spend with friends. What they didn't realize was that an assassin followed them.

When the bus finally stopped, the assassin threw

back the canopy curtains and asked which girl was Malala. He even tried to bargain; he told the rest of the girls that he could shoot Malala alone, or he could shoot all of them. He dared them to give up their friend.

They didn't have to. Malala identified herself, and the shooting began. The assassin fired several times, wounding Malala's friends. As for Malala herself, the assassin shot her in the head and left her for dead. Fortunately, the bullet skimmed the bone of her skull, traveling beneath the skin. She was in danger, but Malala would survive.

The attempt on Malala's life became worldwide news. If the Taliban thought that getting rid of this schoolgirl would solve all their problems, they were very, very wrong. Now, not only did the world know about their plans to squeeze girls out of public life in Pakistan, they knew that they were cowardly enough to try to murder a little girl to achieve that.

Malala flew to the United Kingdom for medical treatment. And there, no one would have blamed her for becoming an anonymous student, earning the education for which she had fought so hard and sacrificed so much.

Instead, as Malala recovered, she put aside her dream to become a doctor. Now she had a much more important mission. If people were willing to kill her to keep her from getting an education, she knew what her life was really for.

Malala Yousafzai is the youngest winner of the Nobel Peace Prize; she didn't give her acceptance speech until she got home from school that day. When she's not in school, she fights for the rights of girls everywhere to get an education. The Taliban thought it would shut her up. Instead, they gave her a worldwide stage.

Now a permanent resident of the United Kingdom, Malala continues her crusade for education. The Taliban tried to stop her from speaking out, and only amplified her voice. Not surprisingly, Malala is not afraid to use it.

Alice Coachman

Alice Coachman

1923–2014

Sometimes, the world is ready for an incredible talent. Sometimes, it's just not.

For Alice Coachman, she was ready at sixteen, winning the first of ten national high jump competitions. She excelled at track and field. Not only did she dominate high jump, Alice also ran away with award after award in the fifty- and one-hundred-meter dashes, and the one-hundred-meter relay. Her athletic skills were so sharp that many people consider her one of the top athletes of all time—yet very few people remember her today.

Why?

As Alice made her ascent to the top of her field, something else overwhelmed the world. In 1938, Europe dissolved into a great war. Germany and Italy allied with each other against France, Great Britain, and Poland. At first, everyone hoped that the war would end quickly. Leaders at the time thought that perhaps if they compromised with German führer Adolf Hitler, they could come to a peaceful solution.

This wasn't to be. Hitler's government was determined to create a perfect society. For them, that meant a society without Jewish people, Romany people, Communists, gays and lesbians, people with disabilities, and more. In fact, to be a "good" German, someone was ideally a member of the Nazi Party, and had blond hair, blue eyes, and an athletic physique. People who didn't fit into this description soon found themselves forced from their homes. They were made to live in ghettos or were imprisoned in concentration camps.

But what does this have to do with Alice Coachman? What does this have to do with sports at all?

Well, the Olympic Games are held every four years. Alice's best shot for claiming her place in history as the finest track-and-field athlete of all time came in 1940 and 1944. Or at least, they should have.

Germany hosted the Olympics in 1936, to much controversy. Athletes of color like Alice were forbidden to live in the Olympic Village. Their presence (and success) were the source of many protests in Berlin at the time. It was an early glimpse of the policies that ultimately led to the creation of concentration and extermination camps.

The next time the Games came around, many countries joined forces to boycott them. They refused to compete with Germany, not while the German government was targeting innocent civilians.

The call for a boycott spread so completely that soon it seemed no one would be at the Games except for Germany. With the world so united against Hitler and his Nazi Party, they all agreed to cancel the Olympics.

Better than many, Alice Coachman understood the injustice of discrimination. She supported the boycott completely, standing in unity with the other athletes who refused to participate. This brave stand unfortunately meant that she missed out on her first two opportunities to compete on the world stage.

She was winning national tournaments—she was the best in the United States, by far. But because of the war, Alice didn't make it to the Olympics until 1948. Though she had missed much of her athletic peak, she still shone.

At those Games, she became the very first African American woman, and the only American woman in 1948, to take gold in an Olympic sport.

Sho Yano

Sho Yano

1993–

There are two ways of becoming a doctor: earning a PhD or a medical degree. No slacker, Sho Yano decided to do both. By the age of twenty-one—no big deal!

When Sho was a toddler, his mother realized that he wasn't like other kids his age. Most two-year-olds are content to hammer pegs through boards and do a little recreational napping. Sho, however, could read himself his own bedtime story.

Then, at the ripe old age of three, he learned to write, as well. Even before preschool, Sho didn't slack. An accomplished pianist by the age of four, he started composing his own music barely a year later.

Of course, for preschool, Sho went to high school. His mother was afraid that his teenage class-mates would hold Sho back. That's why she decided to homeschool him, knocking out elementary, middle, and high school by the age of eight.

At that point, his mom had to admit he needed more schooling than she could provide. Sho scored a fifteen hundred out of sixteen hundred on the SATs, and gained admission to Loyola University. At twelve, he graduated with honors and he still wasn't done!

It was time for Sho to become Dr. Yano. Studying at the University of Chicago, Sho blew through his courses in the Medical Science Training Program. In a remarkably short time, he earned his PhD in molecular genetics—not exactly a breezy course of study.

He capped off his education there with his **dissertation**, Specific Inhibition of Host Processes by Bacteriophage N4 Gene Products. (It's okay if you don't know what all that means—most people don't!)

Now a doctor of philosophy at the age of eighteen, Sho walked directly into his second year of medical school. He'd already mastered molecular genetics. Now he had to learn how to be a physician.

At the same time most people are graduating with their bachelor's degree, Sho finished up medical school and earned his MD. He was the youngest person ever to be granted a medical doctorate in the

University of Chicago's long history. (He doesn't make people call him Doctor Doctor Yano, but he could.)

In case you think Sho's whole life is work, work, work, not so! He makes time for other interests. He still plays the piano, and he has earned a black belt in tae kwon do. And he just recently stopped fighting with his little sister. (He encouraged her to give up her medical studies to follow her passion for music.)

This off-the-IQ-charts child genius is technically no longer a child. He's a young man, putting his degrees to good use practicing medicine. Specifically, practicing pediatric neurology at the University of Chicago.

That's right—this kid wonder rocketed through school at record speeds to become a doctor for kids!

In the 1980s, Ryan White of Kokomo, Indiana, was an ordinary teen who had an unusual disorder: hemophilia. This disease keeps the blood from clotting properly, and requires blood transfusions to stay healthy. During one of these routine transfusions, Ryan was infected with HIV, the virus which causes AIDS.

At the time, the public was terrified of AIDS; worse, most people didn't understand how it spread. People were afraid they might be able to catch HIV/AIDS by shaking someone's hand or drinking from their cup. In a panic, Ryan's middle school expelled him in the middle of the year. If he'd wanted to, Ryan could have stayed quiet and allowed this to play out around him.

Instead, he chose to become an advocate, raising awareness about HIV/AIDS and the truth about living with the condition. Soon, celebrities lent their support to Ryan and his family. When Ryan eventually succumbed to AIDS, he was mourned around the world. His close personal friend, musician Elton John, sang at his funeral—and has carried on his mission ever since.

Selena

Selena
(Selena Quintanilla Perez)
1971–1995

At six years old, Selena Quintanilla already showed the kind of charisma and talent that would make her a star. Born in Texas to Mexican American parents, Selena grew up in Lake Jackson, Texas.

Convinced that she was meant to be a singer, Selena's father created a band for her, Selena y Los Dinos. The other two members of the band were her siblings, so it was a real family affair. They regularly performed in their father's restaurant, and soon, the news spread about this spectacular young artist.

At the age of eleven, Selena (along with Los Dinos) recorded her first album. Her choice of music proved to be controversial at first. Though she wasn't a native speaker of Spanish, she loved to sing Tejano music. (This is a blend of Mexican American, polka, waltzes, and other classical styles of music.)

As she was getting her start, Selena was often denied entry to venues or discriminated against because she was a girl. To some people, Tejano should be performed only by men.

Selena wasn't about to let a bunch of old guys stop her. She continued to record and perform, her audience growing year by year. Soon, she became part of the Tejano music scene, and then a Tejano star.

When she was just fifteen years old, she won Female Vocalist of the Year at the Tejano Music Awards.

Selena was on her way! She signed with a major record label. Introducing Tejano to an English-speaking audience, she managed to cross over to mainstream pop radio stations while still staying true to her musical roots. What's interesting is that initially, Selena didn't even speak Spanish. She had to learn her songs phonetically from her father, though eventually she did become fluent!

Fame growing, Selena was called the Mexican Madonna. One of her most popular singles, "Como La Flor," sold more than three hundred thousand copies when it came out! In 1993, at the age of twenty-two, Selena became the first Tejano artist to win a Grammy Award.

On her very next release, Selena scored four number one hits and started planning for her first English-language album. Excited for the future and newly married, Selena couldn't wait to reach an even wider audience with her music. She was so popular that her parents decided that she needed an official fan club.

Unfortunately, the fan club is what brought a terrible end to Selena's career, and her life. The president of the club started stealing money from the membership fees. When Selena confronted her about it and fired her, the woman shot Selena and killed her. Selena was only twenty-three years old, and she should have had decades more music ahead of her. Instead, her life was cut short by her tragic death.

Nothing, however, can dim her legacy. Her life story was made into a movie starring Jennifer Lopez. On what would have been her fortieth birthday, artists held a tribute concert for her in Houston, Texas. More than sixty-five thousand fans attended the concert, featuring performances by Soraya, Fey, and Gloria Estefan. A recording made of the concert was shown on television—it became the highest-rated Spanish-language program in American television history.

Now, two decades after her death, Selena continues to be one of the most popular Tejano artists of all time.

Shapur II

Shapur II
309–379

History is full of young rulers: three-year-old queens, nine-year-old pharaohs, one-year-old high priests, and ten-year-old emperors. Well, Shapur II of Persia has them all beat. Like . . . super, extra, double, overtime beaten.

See, his father, Shah Hormizd, was the ruler of an empire that stretched from Egypt to Yemen. It was no small nation, and he had plenty of sons waiting to inherit it. The problem was, when there's that much land and power at stake, lots of people want it. And they'll do whatever it takes to get it.

So when Shah Hormizd died, nobles rushed in to make their claim to the throne. Well, sort of. They rushed in to make sure the crown went to someone they thought could be easily controlled. So the nobles murdered Hormizd's eldest son to get him out of the way. But there was a second son waiting in the wings. Oh, oops, nope—the nobles blinded him. Third son's the charm, right? Wrong. The nobles imprisoned him.

That left . . . well, nobody. Except one of Hormizd's wives was pregnant during this tumultuous period. And the nobles figured what better way to influence the king than to raise him from infancy? They rallied around the pregnant woman and crowned her belly—the baby wasn't due for a while yet!

Which means in the race to become the youngest sovereign in the history of the world, Shapur II wins by a mile. What's cool is that despite the nobles' plotting, Shapur II actually became a good king to his people. Persia entered a new golden age, one of prosperity and strength. Shapur II expanded his empire's borders and fended off waves of attacks from the Romans in the East.

His reign was one of the longest in Persian history—literally as long as he lived. For seventy years, Shapur II wore the crown that was originally placed on his pregnant mother's belly. And like his father before him, he had plenty of sons waiting to inherit when he passed, just in case!

Joan of Arc

Joan of Arc
(Jeanne d'Arc)
1412–1431

Born in the little French village of Domrémy, Joan of Arc had a completely ordinary childhood (for a medieval girl in France, that is). She tended to her family's herd of cows. She learned to sew and spin—in fact, she once said she didn't think anyone could best her.*

Deeply religious, she went to Mass, never learned to read, and could only write her name. She had friends in the village; they danced together at church festivals. Sometimes she skipped out on her chores. Often, she was found in the little chapel in town.

It wasn't until Joan turned twelve that things got interesting. One summer day, when she was enjoying the weather, a great burst of light startled her, she said, and she was afraid. Then, there were voices. She didn't recognize them at first.

They encouraged her to go to church. To be a good

girl. Joan's visions wanted her to be the faithful, obedient daughter that she already was. Not so spectacular, huh?

At sixteen, Joan believed the visions had finally given her a mission. A very specific mission: to put Charles VII on the throne once and for all. (In England, the ruling royal family, the Plantagenets, felt they had a rightful claim to the crown of France.)

Pretending that she was going to visit a pregnant cousin, Joan instead went to visit a nearby military garrison. When she got there, she insisted on speaking to the captain. She needed him to escort her to Charles VII. She was going to save the day.

Was the captain impressed? Not even a little. He found her message so ridiculous that he slapped her, then sent her home.

About that time, Joan's parents arranged her marriage. Though Joan met the boy, her mom and dad did all the negotiating.

Nevertheless, she felt as if she'd been called to save France and to crown Charles VII, period. That was her divine mission, and she had to see it through. So when Joan found out that she was engaged, she had no choice:

She disobeyed her parents.

So Joan said, nope, not getting married. And the

boy's parents decided to sue her. The contracts were already signed! Legally, she had to marry her fiancé, they argued. Except, the Church said, she still has to agree to it. If she doesn't agree, then it's not happening.

It didn't happen.

By this time, the war had spilled into Domrémy. Joan agitated to do "something" for the war effort. After Christmas, Joan ran away.

This time, she was determined to make the captain take her seriously. She had specifics now. She needed an escort to Chinon; she had to talk to Charles VII. She was the sign that God was sending; she was the proof that the divine was on France's side.

The captain refused her again (with less slapping, this time). Joan, however, had no intention of giving up. Now, she talked openly about her visions, to anyone who would listen. One of the captain's close friends, Jean de Metz, thought she was an adorable little lunatic. He teased her: sweetie, why are you even here?

She told him, "I must save France, even though I would rather stay home and spin wool with my mother . . . my Lord wills that I do."

Something about that moved de Metz. He believed her; he was the first. He pledged his loyalty to her, and suddenly things moved quickly. With de Metz at her side, the captain finally agreed to talk to her again. The captain's wife sent a message to Chinon about Joan. Would Charles VII consider seeing her?

Charles VII decided better safe than sorry. Maybe Joan was crazy. Maybe she was a divine messenger. The worst thing that could happen was that she would die, and then he wouldn't have to deal with her anymore. The best was that she would lift the English siege on Orléans and make him a king.

So he gave Joan an army to command and sent her into the heart of the war. You get one guess which way the battle for Orléans went. (Spoiler: Joan and her army liberated it; she was seventeen.)

Joan ushered the future king into Reims and attended his coronation. She was pretty snappy about it, too. Out of everybody, she was the only person to bring a battle banner into the church. When somebody asked her why, she said, "It has borne the burden. It was quite right that it receive the honor."

Once on the throne, Charles VII quickly came to consider Joan a liability. She started losing battles. Messengers from God didn't lose. He didn't want anybody thinking that he'd been crowned by accident. So he kind of, sort of let Joan get captured by the English.

The English put her on trial for witchcraft and **heresy**. She answered questions, over and over again, proving she genuinely believed in her mission.

Originally, Joan was charged with seventy counts of heresy. By the time the trial ended, only thirteen charges remained. Those mostly had to do with her wearing men's clothing.

When the court read Joan the letter of confession they crafted for her, she laughed. It wanted her to promise that the voices were gone. She had to go home, wear dresses, and behave.

Joan had never believed she was supposed to fight the whole war by herself. Her mission, to put Charles VII on the throne, was done. The missions after Charles VII's coronation, she even admitted, were carried out at the orders of men, not God. She had no problem agreeing to go home and sin no more.

Unfortunately, it wouldn't be that simple. Before Joan could be sent home, a local lord decided to leave his mark on Joan of Arc. This jerk came to visit her, then tried to assault her in her prison cell.

Furious, Joan put her men's clothing back on. She was much safer in them, and always had been.

Now she realized that she'd never be able to simply go home again. She was too great a prize; she would never be safe. So Joan decided her own fate. She summoned the judges to tell them the voices had decided to speak to her again.

Even now, we don't know what Joan's visions were. The fact is, Joan is the only one who experienced them. Regardless of their actual origin, she believed she was called by God.

That means Joan of Arc wasn't burned at a pillar for turning the war against England. No, Joan of Arc volunteered to be executed. Putting on her battle gear, she deliberately told the church that the voices had returned—breaking her confession. This was her choice; she refused to let the men around her treat her like property.

Just as Joan insisted on charging after her destiny, she ultimately chose her own fate.

That tells us a lot more about Joan of Arc than the pretty legends ever could.

---

* Luckily for her, Athena wasn't around to hear this. Joan of Arc might have found herself turned into a spider, just like Arachne!

ACTIVIST KIDS!

When the city of Chicago decided to close more than fifty schools, primarily in African American neighborhoods, people were infuriated. They protested and they spoke at school board meetings.

When the district ignored the outcry and continued with their plans, one student at Marcus Garvey Elementary became the spokesperson for the entire movement.

Just nine at the time, Asean Johnson was a third-grader with passion. He already planned to become a football player, the president of the United States, a lawyer, and possibly a scientist. He had no idea he would become an activist when he gave a speech about the schools targeted for closure.

Not only did he call out the school district itself, he made it clear that the closing of primarily African American schools was racist. In a speech he wrote himself, Asean pointed out the inequality of the decision. He called out the city's mayor and the school district of Chicago.

Adults cheered as he spoke to the crowd, and when the video of his speech went viral, Asean became a symbol of all the children in Chicago schools. "Education is our right," he declared. "That is why we have to fight!"

Asean's passion made a huge difference for Marcus Garvey Elementary. Though it was slated to be closed, the school system decided to save it after Asean's speech. That, however, still left the students of fifty other schools in need of a champion. No doubt Asean will continue to be that symbol as they all fight for the right to an education.

Sheila Sri Prakash

Sheila Sri Prakash
1955–

Math and science have more than their fair share of prodigies, but the arts are proud to claim Sheila Sri Prakash as their own.

An only child, Sheila got all the advantages and lessons. Painting, music, dance, acting—if there was a lesson for it, she was allowed to take it. She bloomed as an all-around artist. By the age of four, she had mastered Veenai—the classic, stringed instruments that give Indian music its distinctive **timbre**. At the same time, her extraordinary talent as a classical dancer started to draw attention.

When she was only six, she had her public stage debut dancing the Bharata Natyam. Originating in temples more than two thousand years ago, Bharata Natyam is a classical Indian dance. It requires flexibility, grace, and, above all, strength to perform well.

Most students of the dance work for decades to master its details. Sheila's debut at six, however, stunned audiences.

More accomplished than dancers three times her age, Sheila moved with her family from Bhopal to Chennai to further her studies. In addition to Bharata Natyam, Sheila now studied another form of classical dance, Kuchipudi. At the same time, she practiced other art forms as well. Creating sculpture and paintings, honing her skills on the Veenai instruments, Sheila stood out as a prodigy.

At the age of eight, she earned an award for her portrayal of Krishna in the dramatic dance "Nauka Charitram." It was a first for a dancer so young, and she continued to earn lead roles. Year after year, she performed alongside some of the greatest disciples of classical Indian dance. When she wasn't on stage, she was in the recording studio. She played, composed, and recorded with some of the greatest musicians of her age.

At eighteen, Sheila now had a new path in mind for herself. Art, dance, and music filled her life—but now she wanted to go to college to become an architect. This was a controversial decision, indeed. People couldn't believe that this amazing artist wanted to leave dance behind to design buildings. She made this decision in 1973, when many still believed it was wrong for her—a woman—to take a man's place at a university.

Despite the outcry, Sheila went to college anyway. There, she flourished as an architectural student, weaving her history of art and music into her designs. When she graduated, she became one of the first female architects in India. That wasn't enough, however. She was the first woman to build and run her own architecture firm in the country, as well. She has designed thousands of projects and earned some of the highest honors in architecture possible. Named one of the top one hundred architects in the world, Sheila stands apart as a *star*chitect.

That kind of achievement takes grace, good balance, and lots of strength—things that Sheila learned as a dancer when she was just six years old.

Gabby Douglas

Gabrielle "Gabby" Douglas

1995–

The fourth American woman to win in the Olympics' gymnastics all-around competition, and the first woman of color of any nation to do so, Gabby Douglas had a rough march to her amazing victory.

Like most athletes, Gabby started training early. Her older sister Arielle had taken some gymnastics lessons and liked to share her skills. Fascinated by tumbling passes, Gabby watched Arielle carefully and learned to do an aerial (a handless cartwheel). There were plenty of scrapes and falls, but Gabby was determined, and she practiced the move every day, perfecting it with each flip.

Impressed, Arielle talked their mother into letting Gabby, the baby of the family, take lessons. Despite the fact that their single mother had to support four children on her own, she found the way to pay for Gabby's lessons. (Gabby's father wasn't around much, and he didn't help support the family.)

Trying to make the sacrifices worthwhile, Gabby dropped jaws at the gym. New moves came easily to her. She had boundless energy and a passion for gymnastics that practically made her glow. No matter how difficult the move, Gabby was never afraid to try it.

Elite training was hard, but Gabby didn't let that stop her. Unfortunately, she had to overcome other obstacles, as well. For one, she just couldn't seem to stop injuring herself. Once, she had to sit out a whole season with a broken wrist. With the incredible amount of force behind even the simplest of gymnastics moves, Gabby could barely practice.

For another, she stood out as one of only a few African American athletes training at her gym. Some of the other girls bullied her—stealing her clothes from the locker room and singling her out for abuse. A coach suggested that she get a nose job; another athlete joked that Gabby should be their slave and clean up the gym after training.

As much as Gabby loved gymnastics, she hated the way these people treated her. It started eating away at her confidence and poisoning her love of the sport. When she got the chance to change to another coach, Gabby told her mother she wanted to fly out to Iowa to train at his gym. It would be a fresh start, in a new place, with a coach she trusted.

At first, Gabby's mother balked. But then Gabby told her that she either had to leave or had to quit gymnastics. And that's how Gabby ended up, at the age of fourteen, flying to Des Moines to train.

It was hard to leave her mom and her siblings behind in Virginia. Worse still, she injured her hip shortly after arriving in Iowa, which kept her from competing. Taking the downtime and making it useful, Gabby worked on developing her arms and her abs to improve her performance on the uneven bars.

Though Gabby was surrounded by other serious athletes, and her foster family took good care of her, she was homesick. Many times, she considered quitting gymnastics so she could go back home to Virginia. But the promise of the 2012 Olympics in London loomed in her future. She'd come too far and sacrificed too much to get there. She at least had to try to make the team. Her ambition wouldn't let her do anything less.

What's interesting is that Gabby did make the U.S. Women's Olympics gymnastics team—but no one expected much of her. She'd been injured so often that her training had been erratic. She was good, but not a standout going into the Games. For many people, she didn't fit the image of an all-American gymnast.

That all changed when Gabby swept the all-around artistic competition.

Suddenly, everyone's eyes turned to Gabby. She stunned the crowds with her athleticism and her strength. The nickname one of her coaches had given her, the Flying Squirrel, was on the lips of every Olympics fan. Gabby wasn't done in London. Next, she did her part to help the American team win team gold—for the first time in sixteen years.

Even after winning Olympic gold, things haven't been perfect for Gabby. She didn't compete in 2013, and she's moved among several coaches. Some were afraid to take her on because she was too accomplished. Others didn't want to offend the coach she'd just left. But as of 2015, Gabby's working on her comeback.

She plans to be the first African American woman to win all-around gold twice. She hopes that 2016 will be her best year yet!

OLYMPIC KIDS

Throughout the history of the games, some really young people have broken records, taken home medals, and become legends in their sport.

Nadia Comaneci—At fourteen years old, Nadia won gold in the women's all-around gymnastics competition in the 1976 games in Montreal. She was the youngest ever to take that prize, and the first gymnast ever to earn a perfect 10.

Krisztina Egerszegi—Also fourteen years old, this Hungarian swimmer took the world record as youngest gold medalist swimmer from Kusuo Kitamura, when she swam to victory in the 1988 Seoul Games.

Tara Lipinski—Just fifteen years old at the 1998 Nagano Games, Tara upset favorite Michelle Kwan to win in ladies' individual figure skating—the youngest ladies' gold medalist in that category ever!

Dimitrios Loundras—Only ten years old, Dimitrios won bronze in the 1896 Athens Games in gymnastics. He's still the youngest winner ever.

Fu Mingxia—At thirteen, Fu captured gold in ladies' springboard diving at the 1992 Barcelona Games. Four years later, she repeated the feat at the 1996 Atlanta Games.

Maria Gaetana Agnesi

Maria Gaetana Agnesi

1718–1799

A child prodigy, Maria Gaetana Agnesi revolution-
ized mathematics—but all she wanted to do was join
a convent.

Born to a wealthy Milanese family in 1718, Maria
and her siblings (she was the oldest of twenty-one!)
all enjoyed an extensive education. Tutors from the
church taught them music, mathematics, science, philosophy, and more. From an early age, it was obvious
Maria was no average scholar.

Fluent in French by five years old, Maria added
Hebrew, Greek, and Latin to the mix by the age of
nine. By thirteen, she'd mastered Spanish and German as well. Her father's learned friends called her
the Seven Tongued **Orator**.

And how did her father's friends know about
Maria's gift for language? She attended salons with

them—meetings where people gave speeches, debated philosophies, or discussed a particular topic. Shy Maria didn't enjoy attending salons. Nevertheless, at her father's insistence, she gave many impressive speeches and **dissertations** there.

At an early age, Maria realized that most girls weren't getting an education like she was. Her family's riches, and her father's love of education, gave Maria a very different life from most of her peers.

While Maria studied mathematics, most girls didn't. Their tutors focused on music, sewing, social graces (a fancy way of saying "being pretty and pleasant"), and morals. Their training didn't encourage them to think or explore. They were training to find a husband!

How unfair, Maria thought. With the help of a tutor, she wrote a passionate speech about girls' rights to an education. Then, she translated it into Latin— the language of education in the eighteenth century— and memorized it. At the next salon, she delivered this speech with conviction.

Maria was just nine at the time.

Combining oration and philosophy, Maria wrote *Propositiones Philosophicae* in her teens. A collection of arguments and observations about philosophy and natural sciences, the book drew rave reviews.

People came from all over Europe to discuss Maria's essays with her. It was a big achievement, but it embarrassed Maria. She said she didn't want to bore people. More likely, she remained shy and disliked the attention.

Maria had a keen mind for mathematics. Delving into algebra and geometry, she soon found herself solving **ballistics** problems and writing about differential calculus. Because she spoke so many languages, she could read papers about math from all over the world.

This gave Maria an understanding of math that most people didn't have. It also gave her leverage with her father. When she was twenty, instead of looking for a husband, she decided to join a convent.

Horrified, her father refused to let her go. When her mother passed away, Maria made a deal with her father. She would care for her siblings and teach them physics and math, if he would let her retire from public life.

Her father agreed, reluctantly. Set free from social obligations, Maria finally found her peace. At home, she no longer had to participate in salons and thesis defenses. Instead, she got to devote herself to studying math, science, and religion full time.

She wrote several **treatises** on mathematics, including the thousand-page *Analytical Institutions.* It started out as a textbook for her siblings, but it stunned and thrilled the scientific world when she published it. It was the very first complete examination of math concepts, made possible by Maria's gift for language.

Most people are only starting their careers at the age of twenty. Instead, Maria Gaetana Agnesi retired. Though she continued to write and publish, eventually she gave up mathematics entirely. Instead, she opened her home to the poor and dedicated herself to service.

Years later, when her father passed away and her siblings were all grown, Maria finally got her wish. Though she was one of the greatest minds in mathematics and physics, Maria spent the rest of her life in quiet contemplation as a nun.

Bonus Fact!

Maria Agnesi didn't just write the comprehensive book of mathematics—she also became part of it. In her text, she described a certain curve as *versieri*, which means "turn" in Italian. Some pun-loving dude who translated her book realized that sounded a lot like aversieri—witch. So when he wrote about the turn in English, he named it the *Witch of Agnesi*. That's what it's called to this day!

Marc Márquez

Marc Márquez
1993–

How fast do you like to go? Marc Márquez's answer is "as fast as possible." He's a motorcycle racer in the Moto Grand Prix, and one of the youngest winners ever!

Marc started out fast. Born just outside Barcelona, Spain, in a town called Cervera, Marc got his very first motorbike when he was four years old. It was something he begged for. Proof that his parents were incredibly supportive from the beginning: they're the ones who bought it for him! They loved to watch Marc tackle top speeds with nothing between him and the road but a helmet and a racing suit.

At eight years old, he won the Catalan title—a big boost for a young athlete. Experimenting, Marc tried out lots of different kinds of tracks. He wanted to find the perfect course for him. Naturally, he gravitated toward off-road. Why? Because he could go faster! Just one year after taking the Catalan title, Marc debuted in league racing and came in third. He was on his way.

Pretty soon, Marc was gobbling up all the titles. When he was ten, he won the Open Race 50. At eleven, Marc found mentors and partners in the Montlau racing family. They took him under their wing, making him feel like a part of the family. The training and advice he got from them was invaluable. More serious than ever about racing, Marc focused all his training on speed, speed, and more speed.

The practice and determination paid off. Growing and maturing as a motorbike racer, Marc joined the Spanish motorcycling championship when he was just fifteen years old. In Jerez, an extremely famous and well-storied track in MotoGP, Marc took his very first victory. The youngest rider ever to accomplish this, the world couldn't help but take notice.

Marc even said, after that, things got even faster. Since 2008, Marc has moved up the ladder in his sport. He's famous for his incredibly low, tight turns. If you watch him race, you'll be amazed. Sometimes he gets so low, his knee skims the ground. It's breathtaking to watch, and death defying to accomplish. That said, more than once, Marc has dipped a little too low and crashed himself right out of competition.

He always gets back up again. And in 2010, his speed and spirit brought him to the very top. At seventeen, he raced and won the world championship. Number one in the world—Marc says that this was his happiest moment, ever. No wonder—he was beating out other racers in their twenties and thirties, living his dream.

As of this writing, Marc Márquez is twenty-two. He's suffered a few injuries and missed the podium a time or two, but he continues to get back on his bike every time. There are still races to win and titles to earn. And if history is any indication, Marc will be doing both—as fast as possible!

Okita Soji

Okita Soji
1844–1868

It's supposed to take an entire lifetime to master a martial art like Tennen Rishin-ryu. For Okita Soji, that was true—but his life was just a short twenty-five years.

Okita was a prodigy. Born of a samurai family, he was already destined for great things. At the age of nine, he moved into the Tennen Rishin-ryu dojo (a martial arts school) to study under the master Kondo Shusuke. Focused on nothing but the martial art, Okita conquered one technique after the next.

At eighteen years old, Okita earned the license of total transmission—the final, highest rank of accomplishment. In eight short years, Okita had mastered all twenty-three techniques, passed all his tests, and was fully qualified to take students of his own. Most masters needed at least thirty years to achieve this.

If that were all we knew about Okita, that alone would be remarkable. However, the part he played in Japanese history has made him both a legend and a folk hero.

At the time, Japan was a country governed by a group of military leaders called the Shogun, who were technically appointed by the emperor. However, the Shogun were the ones who waged war, raised taxes, and negotiated with other countries. By the nineteenth century, their power almost eclipsed the emperor's.

But only almost. The emperor stepped in, stripping the Shogun of some of their traditional might. These long-standing governors were pushed out of Kyoto, and those who remained needed protection. That's where the Shinsengumi—and Okita Soji— came in.

The Shinsengumi was a special police force. In its ranks were people with extraordinary heritage and training. Okita was among them, and was considered one of the finest sword masters in all Japan. He had a signature technique, Mumyo-Ken, the unenlightened blade. Legend had it that with this technique, Okita could strike three places at once.

That would have been very handy when it came to political **assassinations**—one of the things the Shinsengumi carried out for the Shogun. Unfortunately, even as Okita was elevated to the fifth master of Tennen Rishin-ryu, his life was fading. No one is entirely sure when Okita contracted tuberculosis.

What is certain, however, is that he died at the age of twenty-five, alone in an Edo hospital. His body was buried later that night. Today, his grave is a private shrine, open only on a single June day each year to celebrate his legacy.

Because Okita was such a prodigy, he captured the imaginations of many young Japanese people. His story has been told and retold in popular novels, in films, even in anime, manga, and video games. Sometimes, he's reimagined as a vampire or a vengeful spirit. Sometimes, he plays the young, idealistic hero, bound by loyalty to the end.

Always, he's portrayed with a sword; almost always he dies a tragic hero.

These days, it's hard to figure out where the line between history and legend blurs with Okita Soji. But what better legacy than immortality for the youngest master in the history of Tennen Rishin-ryu?

Philo T. Farnsworth

Philo T. Farnsworth
1906–1971

Quick! Explain how a television works!

Well, yeah, plug it in, turn it on, blah blah blah. But think about it: How does the television really work? How do the pictures get from the TV or movie studio and onto your screen?

How can images filmed in Tunisia in 1976, when nobody had ever heard of Star Wars, appear in your living room today (but probably edited down to fit the movie and commercials into a two-hour slot)?

If your answer included fusing together thousands of tiny dots in rapid succession, well done! You know what Philo T. Farnsworth figured out all the way back in 1920. Philo was kind of a mad genius, minus the mad part. He was always coming up with new ideas and inventions.

Fascinated by electricity, Philo was stoked when

his parents moved to a new farm that had it. He spent a lot of time breaking down machines and putting them back together to figure out how they worked.

For example, he hooked his mom's hand-cranked clothes washer up to an electric motor: voilà—instant Laundromat! Broken generator? No problem—Philo could fix it. He even won twenty-five dollars for inventing a magnetic car lock. (In today's money, that's about three hundred bucks!)

Now, people had already come up with the idea of sending images through the air. The problem was getting a whole picture onto hundreds of screens, all at the same time. The available technology worked, but poorly. The problem fascinated Philo; he wanted to solve it.

Philo pondered the question every day. It buzzed in his brain, demanding attention. One afternoon, he was working his family's farm. Rumbling along on his plow, he couldn't help but stare at the long, straight rows he made in the earth. They lined up perfectly, but he still recognized the field.

Suddenly, Philo had a realization.

Sending a whole image all at one time was the problem! If he could just break the image down into parts, he'd only have to send a little bit at a time. So Philo sketched out his ideas for a new invention: an image dissector. Instead of trying to send a whole picture, Philo wanted to send something a lot smaller: an electron. Televisions would have long, straight rows made up of tiny dots—pixels.

His technology required only that broadcast signals tell televisions either to turn on a pixel or to leave it dark. When all the dots are collected in one place, they create a picture. When you send a series of pictures in rapid succession, the image appears to move.

Philo understood that the human brain could reassemble these dots lightning fast. People moving pictures—video! And he was right! He patented his idea. At the time, it sounded like crazy, mystical magic. But it wasn't. It was science.

What's amazing is that he saw it all before it existed. In one spark! In one afternoon, plowing a field and thinking about the rows. I mean, when I asked you to explain how a television worked, you could have Googled the answer. But Philo came up with it all by himself. No wonder we call him visionary!

Melba Liston

Melba Liston
1926–1999

Melba Liston was not interested in what other people thought she could do.

A trombone is a very big instrument. In fact, it was about as big as Melba was, when she fell in love with one at the age of seven. She'd never seen anything more beautiful, and who could argue with that? A whorl of gleaming brass, full of intricate loops and spirals, the giant trombone whispered to her. She felt like they were meant to be together.

Her teachers discouraged her. To play a trombone, the musician has to extend the slide to seven positions. And that slide, when fully extended, can be up to nine feet long. Even though she was tall for her age, she wasn't that tall! In fact, she had a tough time hitting the sixth and seventh positions with the slide. But so what? She knew if she practiced hard enough (and grew a little more) that she'd be hitting those notes in no time.

And she was! Just one year later, Melba had accomplished so much on her trombone that she was invited to play solos on the local radio station. She was an eight-year-old musical genius, with a real flair for coaxing the most beautiful music out of her giant trombone. It was obvious that Melba had a very special gift.

When she was eleven, her mother moved the family from St. Louis to Los Angeles. There, she found Melba a full-time music teacher named Alma Hightower. In the years between eleven and sixteen, Melba learned a lot in her lessons. So much so that when she turned sixteen, she decided that it was time for her to become a professional musician.

Joining the musicians union, Melba soon found a job as part of the Lincoln Theatre's house band. She loved it—and she discovered something else that she loved to do at the same time. In her teens at the Lincoln Theatre, Melba started composing and arranging music, too. She had a knack for jazz, and a real ear for exciting, complicated melodies and rhythms.

Very few women broke through in jazz as a composer. Melba was often the only woman in the room and frequently the only one in the credits. In this mostly male environment, Melba often found it tough to keep going. The work wasn't hard—she loved music. What was hard was the way the male musicians abused her, physically and verbally. It would have been better to be ignored or overlooked. Instead, they liked to bully her and tried to break her down.

This wasn't the only hardship, either. Because Melba was African American, living in a time when the United States was still a very segregated society, she often found it difficult just being allowed to perform. Even if she could play in whites-only clubs, she wasn't allowed to stay in those hotels. Between racism and sexism, Melba had a hard time doing the thing she loved most.

She persevered, because her love of music was greater than the disappointments in the people around her. Eventually, she stopped playing in the band, but she never stopped writing and arranging music. Other artists called her visionary.

When each new style came into vogue, Melba was already there—she combined jazz with Afrobeat and Motown. Her compositions were complicated and compelling. People loved playing Melba's music, and they still do, to this day. Though she never quite reached the level of fame she deserved during her lifetime, musicians everywhere today consider her an inspiration.

And what an inspiration! It doesn't get any more encouraging than to look at an instrument that's taller than you, bigger than you, and to decide to tame it anyway. Melba did all that, and more.

Making History, Changing the World

In the 1930s, Adolf Hitler's Nazi Party took root in Germany. Winning elections and taking over political posts, they soon had control of the entire country.

To ensure they kept that control, the Nazis created Hitlerjugend—the Hitler Youth. Everyone between the ages of ten and seventeen was encouraged to join. (Eventually, they were legally required to join—and if their parents refused, their children were taken from them.)

The Hitler Youth were kind of like the Scouts, but this was a very dark version. Part of their activities included spying on church groups and breaking up Jewish-owned businesses.

For kids who wanted to actively rebel against the Hitler Youth, the Swingkinder (Swing Kids) waited with open arms. They'd started out as just a bunch of fans of jazz and swing music (which were forbidden). They liked to swing dance (also forbidden), they didn't like politics (definitely not cool with the Nazi Party), and they really related to British and American fashions (so totally forbidden, it's not even funny).

At first, they gathered just in protest. Why shouldn't they be allowed to listen to the music they liked? What was so wrong with dancing the jitterbug? Soon, however, it was impossible to ignore the grave changes the Nazi Party brought to Germany. Certain kinds of art, jazz music, dancing, and more were now illegal for everyone. On top of that, Jewish people were no longer allowed their freedom.

And what began as a protest against authority turned into a movement. Soon, the Swing Kids started organizing politically. Instead of Sieg Heil, the Nazi salute, they'd respond with Swing Heil! They joined forces with resistance movements, helping the war effort against the Nazis whenever they could.

Eventually, the Nazis made it illegal to be a Swing Kid at all. To be recognized in a "zoot suit" instead of an HJ uniform was considered treason. The Nazis added Swing Kids to the long list of people they arrested and shipped to concentration camps during World War II.

The Hitlerjugend and the Swingkinder embodied the conflict in Europe in miniature. They were opposing forces, battling for control of an otherwise uncertain future. Ultimately, the Hitlerjugend, like Hitler and the Nazi Party, were disbanded.

The Swingkinder who survived the concentration camps or escaped persecution grew up. They had kids of their own. And that generation became the peace-loving hippies and flower children of the 1960s. (Proof that kids are always the ones with the power to change the world!)

Anne Frank

Anne Frank
1929–1945

Don't feel guilty reading Anne Frank's diary.

When Anneliese Frank first started writing in her wartime red-and-white-checkered journal, it was just for her. She needed to express herself in the midst of very frightening times. The German Nazi Party had banned Jewish people from attending schools, going to shops, seeing movies—basically, living their lives.

Worse, they'd started removing Jewish people from their homes. Some, they installed in **ghettos**. Others, they transported to concentration camps. Healthy prisoners were worked to death; sick ones were put to death immediately.

The Frank family had already fled Nazi persecution in Germany, starting a new life in the Netherlands. They considered fleeing to the United States, to Israel—to a lot of places.

Before they could, however, the Nazis invaded the Netherlands, as well. Anne Frank and her family were trapped. Soon thereafter, the elder Frank daughter, Margot, was called to go to a work camp.

The family decided to disappear into a "Secret Annex" inside Mr. Frank's business building. They hid there with four other people, the van Pels family and Friedrich Pfeffer. Those names probably don't sound familiar, and there's a good reason for that.

Anne created pseudonyms for everyone in the Annex. In her diary, she wrote about the Van Daans (really the van Pels) and Albert Dussel (really Friedrich Pfeffer). She even gave her own family new names. She wanted to be Anne Robin; she named her sister Betty Robin; her parents, Frederick and Nora.

For just a diary, their identities didn't matter. But after a radio address by the Dutch cabinet minister Gerrit Bolkestein, Anne realized that she wasn't just writing a diary anymore.

Minister Bolkestein encouraged ordinary people—pastors with sermons, letter writers, diary keepers—to collect their writings. There had to be a bigger record, a personal record, of what happened during that war. He said, "History cannot be written on the basis of official decisions and documents alone."

Anne felt as if he was talking to her, personally. That day, she started rewriting her diary. Sometimes she took out details she felt were too personal. Sometimes, she added more detail when she thought it was important. And yes, she changed everyone's names to protect their privacy.

Sadly, Anne never finished the rewrite. On August 4, 1944, Nazi soldiers invaded the Secret Annex. Everyone was arrested, Anne's papers scattered, the Secret Annex shattered.

After the arrest, Miep Gies returned to the hidden room to collect their belongings. She'd been helping them hide all along, and now she felt responsible for the few things they had left. It was she who found Anne's writings and short stories. Carefully, she packed them all up and returned them to Anne's father after the war ended.

In fact, the original 1943 diary was never found. However, Anne's published diary had no gap for that year because she was preparing it for publication. She personally revised the version of her 1943 diary that we read today.

The last entry Anne revised was March 29,

1944. After her arrest, the Nazis transported Anne, her mother, and Margot to a series of concentration camps. First, to Westerbork in the Netherlands, then to Auschwitz in Poland—where Anne's mother died. Finally, Anne and Margot made their final journey, to Bergen-Belsen.

There, she and Margot succumbed to **typhus**. Margot first, then Anne. Though records are sparse, new evidence suggests they both passed away in February, two months before the Allies liberated the camp.

Anne Frank was only fifteen years old—but her voice still rings out from the Holocaust. Though Anne's red-checkered book started as a diary, it became an indelible reminder of the humanity, and the humanity lost, during one of Europe's darkest periods.

Pocahontas

Pocahontas
(Matoaka)
1595–1617

You've probably heard of Pocahontas. Seen animated movies about her, learned a version of her story in your social studies class. How she threw herself on top of Captain John Smith to keep her father from dashing his brains out. It's fantastic stuff, a great legend.

And that's probably all it is.

Let's talk about the real Pocahontas. Her father, Wahunsunacock, was an Algonquian Powhatan—a paramount chief. He led a coalition of about twenty-eight tribes in a place we now call Virginia. He wasn't a king or an emperor, which means Pocahontas wasn't a princess.

And oh yeah, her real name was Matoaka. Pocahontas was a nickname. It means naughty.

So anyway, Pocahontas and pretty much the rest of her people were initially interested in the English. They didn't know if they were visitors or settlers. It seemed a little odd that these guys didn't plant crops even though they seemed to be starving.

From other encounters with the English, the Powhatan knew they had guns, textiles, and steel. What he didn't know was whether members of this group were friends or foes. He dealt with them, but carefully.

When the starving English came to them for food, Powhatan opened a trade relation with them. He offered them oysters, corn, and fish, in exchange for iron hatchets and copper tools.

So Pocahontas's father had already met Captain John Smith. He treated the English like another tribe—one they could war with, or one with whom they could share peace. More often than not, the English picked war.

For example. Smith decided to take a band of men deep into Algonquian territory in search of a shortcut to the ocean. The Pacific Ocean. (Dude had no idea where he was, obviously.) Now remember, the English were being treated as an allied tribe at the time. Well, Smith tromped right into other tribes' territory and got smacked down for it.

They captured Smith and took him to Powhatan. And this is where Pocahontas's myth should start, except . . . a few weeks after his capture, Smith wrote to friends about the incident.

Did he write about the selfless chief's daughter who saved his life?* Nope. He said at the time that he was scared, but the Algonquian treated him very well. He got a chance to learn some of their language, and then Powhatan set him free. Pocahontas was there and certainly met him, but she goes unmentioned by Smith in his letter.

This was the beginning of Pocahontas's dealings with the English. She visited Jamestown and played with the children there. Making friends, getting to know Smith—Pocahontas was a curious twelve-year-old who wanted to find out more about her new neighbors.

Then, in 1609, the English told Pocahontas that Smith had died. Actually, he'd been injured and sent back to England. But Pocahontas felt as if she'd lost a friend. Perhaps she had; unfortunately, the English saw her only as an opportunity.

Jamestown soon found itself starving again. In order to get the supplies they needed for the colony, they tricked Pocahontas into boarding an English supply ship. They made her their prisoner and tried to ransom her. They wanted food, guns, and the Englishmen who had been captured. Those were their demands.

Well, Powhatan released the English and sent food, but he ignored the request for guns. Pocahontas remained a prisoner.

By this point, Pocahontas was pretty ticked. She was mad at her dad for leaving her captive. But she was just as mad at the English for capturing her. She thought they'd been friends; now she realized she was just a pawn in a political game.

Held captive for over a year, Pocahontas watched the war between her people and the English rage. Perhaps her father didn't realize it, but she was sure: the English were there to stay. If her nation was going to survive, they had to come to some kind of lasting peace.

So to free herself and to end the war, Pocahontas agreed to marry a tobacco farmer named John Rolfe. This would unite the English and her people. She spent the entire year in Jamestown, learning English, and living among them.

That marriage was called the Peace of Pocahontas, and it lasted for eight years. In fact, it lasted longer than Pocahontas herself. She traveled to England with her new husband and became quite the celebrity. Everyone was fascinated by her; she even met King James.

And that's when Captain John Smith rolled out of the woodwork. Now that Pocahontas was famous, he wanted to be associated with her. He met with her—surprise, I'm not dead!

Pocahontas was furious. She'd shown him friendship, and he hadn't even bothered to tell her he was alive? That was the last time Pocahontas and John Smith ever spoke. He didn't start telling the salvation story until after Pocahontas died—which she did, at twenty-two.

So there was a chief's daughter (nick)named Pocahontas. And she did create (temporary) peace between the English and the Powhatan Confederation. But she did it with politics and diplomacy, when she was fifteen. Not raw with emotion for a man she loved (because she was eleven at the time and Smith was a stranger to her).

Her real story is much greater than that. She alone brokered peace between two nations. For her, at least, it lasted the rest of her life.

* In fact, the captain told this same story three times, about three different girls. So either John Smith was a total seventeenth-century rock star whom girls all over the world couldn't get enough of, or he was making stuff up. Reader, you can decide.

Duke Kahanamoku

Duke Kahanamoku

1890–1968

Though he wasn't royalty, Duke Kahanamoku became the king of swimming and surfing as a young athlete.

The eldest of nine children, Duke was not the studious one. School didn't interest him, the water did. He spent hours and hours on the beaches of Waikiki when he was growing up, perpetually bronzed by the sun and forever covered in seawater. As a teen, he regularly swam times that beat world records.

The thing was, he couldn't get those records into the books because he was just one guy on a beach in Hawaii. The Amateur Athletic Union required a formal organization to time records, so at the age of eighteen, Duke formed the Hui Nalu Canoe Club. It was the "club of the waves," and despite the name, most everyone who participated were swimmers. (They enjoyed surfing and canoeing, too!)

Even though Duke now had the formal organization, the Amateur Athletic Union still couldn't believe that Duke swam his reported times. In 1911, he headed out for another formal time test of the one-hundred-meter freestyle. In the open ocean, battling currents and wind, Duke's swim took almost five seconds off the official world record. Then he broke two more world records for good measure.

In disbelief, the AAU refused to acknowledge the record-beating swim. According to them, the judges hadn't timed the runs properly. And Duke was aided by the ocean currents. And quite possibly, the race course wasn't as long as it was supposed to be. Duke waited while they measured the course four times. He was ultimately deemed the winner of the race. But they refused to acknowledge his new world records.

Their explanation was that they didn't think any human being could swim that fast. They were about to get schooled.

In 1912, Duke moved to the United States (Hawaii would not become a state until 1959) to train and practice for the Olympics. He made the U.S. Swimming Team and flew to Stockholm to compete in the 1912 Games.

He took gold in the one-hundred- and four-hundred-meter freestyle events, and broke two world records in the process. There was no controversy this time. Now no one could deny that Duke was the fastest swimmer in the world! His technique, a combination of a flutter kick and a scissor kick, fascinated fans. His kick was so strong that it lifted his body out of the water as he swam.

This gave Duke such speed and stability that soon other freestyle swimmers adopted his style. Today, the Kahanamoku kick is considered the baseline for all freestyle swimming athletes. After earning gold in Sweden, Duke became a regular at the Olympics. More gold and more broken records followed in 1920, 1924, and 1932. In fact, he didn't give up the gold until 1932, but he didn't feel bad about taking second place to Johnny Weissmuller.

Weissmuller became an actor, and later famously portrayed Tarzan on the silver screen. Duke always liked to joke that it took Tarzan to beat him in the water.

Duke spent the rest of his life swimming, surfing, and sharing his love of the water with the world. He left behind his legacy in the Kahanamoku kick, and in long board surfing. And when he passed away in 1968, his family did the only thing that seemed right:

They buried him at sea.

Elagabalus

Elagabalus
204–222

If you're looking for a role model, you'd choose Elagabalus, boy emperor of Rome, only if you wanted to be bad. Very, very bad. Wicked, even.

Born Varius Avitus Bassianus, Elagabalus inherited the family business: high priest to the Syrian god El-Gabal (aka Baal). No big deal, he was just the religious leader of all of Syria while he was still in diapers. He took the job seriously (as soon as, you know, he learned to walk and talk). He wanted to raise El-Gabal above all other gods—and it just so happened that Julia Maesa, Elagabalus's grandma, had some ambitious plans for him, as well.

She spread a rumor that Elagabalus was the son of beloved Emperor Caracalla. (He totally wasn't, but that's okay. A good rumor can go a long way!) And it just so happened that the Roman people were pretty ticked off with Macrinus, the current emperor. See, he used to be Caracalla's bodyguard. Um, until he snuck up on Caracalla while he was visiting a temple and stabbed him to death.

The Roman people seemed to agree that Elagabalus was the rightful heir and decided to make him emperor. (Grandma Julia laughed a wicked laugh and watched from the sidelines.) Because why not? Fourteen-year-old emperors never hurt anybody. Except, they did. All the time. And Elagabalus wouldn't be any different.

Because he was the supreme ruler of the largest empire in the world. They may as well have crowned him president of the entire planet. He could do anything he wanted, and he did. The Romans of Rome had their own gods and, for the most part, were content to let other people enjoy theirs as they saw fit. Well, Elagabalus ended that when he brought the Black Stone of Baal to Rome and built a temple for it.

This two-ton black meteorite was a holy object for the Syrians. They believed that it was the physical representation of Baal on earth. It wasn't just a symbol to them. The meteorite was Baal. They dressed it in gold and silks, and they moved it through their kingdom on a great, golden chariot.

If you can't tell, the Syrians and the Romans had a special kind of relationship with their gods. Their gods, though only existing in spirit, possessed some human qualities, according to legend. For instance, Jupiter loved the ladies (which ticked off his wife, Juno); Mars had a lousy temper, which fit with being a god of war. And Minerva—she was battle-ready and wise.

The Romans didn't consider their gods good role models. The gods were just in charge, and the best their people could do was try to win their favor with sacrifices, favors, and praise. Or at the very least, they tried really hard not to tick them off. Insult Jupiter and you might get struck by lightning, after all.

So, when Elagabalus brought the Black Stone of Baal to Rome, he was making sure he didn't make his main man Baal mad. First step, don't tick off your god! But Elagabalus was looking for more than that— he wanted Baal's favor. So even though the Romans were cool with adding gods, they were shocked when Elagabalus declared that Jupiter was no longer the number one god in Rome. From here on out, it would be Baal—and he drove the stone god right up to the Coliseum and built a shrine for him.

Then, to make an official alliance with Baal and

the Roman gods, Elagabalus decided to marry Baal to one of the Roman goddesses. Since he was both emperor and priest, his word was law. If he said that Baal was getting married, then he was getting married.

Elagabalus chose Baal's bride very, very carefully. Only Minerva would do—she was a goddess of wisdom and battle, so it was a perfect match. Except for the fact, of course, that Minerva, chose to remain a virgin. Unlike her fellow gods, she was more concerned with wisdom than romance. That didn't matter to Elagabalus.

Oh, but it mattered to the Romans. It mattered so much that they rioted in the streets. Then, as if people weren't angry enough, Elagabalus decided he personally would marry one of the Vestal Virgins—the sacred untouched priestesses. The ones who, legendarily, tended the eternal flame that kept Rome under the protection of the goddess Vesta. It was against the law even to touch a Vestal, let alone marry one.

But hey, Elagabalus wasn't just any old citizen. He was a high priest! The emperor! And easily bored. He married his Vestal, then set her aside a year later. Around the same time, he gave up on the idea of marrying El-Gabal to Minerva (probably because he didn't want to end up like Caracalla, dead, with a bodyguard's dagger in his back).

Instead, he married his god to a lesser Roman goddess to keep the peace. Much to the Romans' irritation, however, he never gave up his ceremonial duties as a high priest. All day long, he sacrificed sheep and goats to El-Gabal. Some Romans complained that he sacrificed little boys, too—but that was probably just a slanderous rumor . . . probably.

Okay, so Elagabalus was kind of a jerk. And self-centered. Definitely a sheep sacrificer, if not worse. To be fair, Roman emperors were famous for their quirks, but Elagabalus took it a step further. It wasn't enough for him to marry Vestal Virgins, divorce them, take them back, then take new wives as it suited his fancy. Nope. You could also find him playing hide-and-seek in the imperial villa with his bodyguard. And if you couldn't find him, there was probably a good reason for that. He also liked to go out in disguises to flirt with visitors to the city.

Now, Elagabalus wasn't stupid. He realized that people didn't like him. Unfortunately, his grandma Julia was the one who'd engineered his regency. She was the true power behind the empire. Since she couldn't change li'l Elagabally (some high priests of El-Gabal just can't be tamed), she figured out a way to put the brakes on his chariot crash of a reign.

Grandma Julia conned him into naming a thirteen-year-old cousin, Alexianus, his heir. It would be great, she told him. Alexianus can do all the boring political work! You can spend more time throwing goats in El-Gabal's fire! At first, Elagabalus agreed to this. But soon he realized he was losing his power over Rome. How to fix that? **Assassinate** Alexianus, of course.

Unfortunately, Elagabalus was better at dispatching sheep than successors. The palace guards foiled his assassination attempts over and over. Finally, Grandma Julia got sick of trying to keep Elagabalus under her thumb. She arranged for his troops to kill him at the first opportunity.

He died a little like his alleged father: stabbed in the back by people he should have been able to trust. But here's a hint that the Roman plotters and planners were way madder at him than they were Caracalla. After his murder, Caracalla was celebrated as a great emperor and deeply mourned.

Elagabalus? Well, he was slaughtered and beheaded. And then, the Romans dragged the pieces of his body through the streets of the city in celebration. Then, then! They dumped his remains in the Tiber River, to be nommed by fish for all eternity. If that wasn't enough to clarify their displeasure, the Romans had one more final indignity for their wicked boy emperor: they tore down El-Gabal's temple and sent the Black Stone back to Syria.

Yep, they kicked his god out of Rome. Take that, Elagabalus!

Venus Williams

Serena Williams

Venus and
Serena Williams
1980– and 1981–

Born in Saginaw, Michigan, and relocated to Compton, California, Venus and Serena Williams started playing tennis early.

A five-year-old Venus and a four-year-old Serena proved to be quick studies on the Compton court. Trained by their parents, the sisters had a strength and athleticism unusual for their ages. Their potential was so great, the Williams family decided to move to Florida, when the girls were nine and ten. They enrolled Venus and Serena in a training academy, and they started playing tennis on the juniors circuit.

The wins poured in. The Williams sisters played both singles (by themselves) and doubles (as a team). In less than a year, they had climbed to the top of the charts. Venus was rated the number one juniors player under twelve in Florida and Serena earned the number one juniors player under ten. The Williams sisters were a hurricane, storming their way to victory everywhere they played.

Some people couldn't handle their success. Whispers crossed the court: white parents complaining about the African American sisters ruining the sport. Critics dismissed the way they played, saying the Williams sisters had nothing to offer but brute strength.

Though the Williams sisters had been at the training academy, their parents remained their coaches. And the coaches had had enough. It was important for them to see their daughters succeed—but also to be little girls. Unwilling to tolerate the racism against their daughters on the juniors circuit, the Williams family withdrew from competition completely.

An unprecedented move, it seemed that Venus and Serena had peaked as tennis players. After all, how could they be expected to grow into mature athletes on the adult tennis circuit if they didn't continue playing through the ranks in the juniors? Well, it turns out that they did just fine. Better than fine, actually.

Just because they weren't competing on the circuit didn't mean they weren't competing. Venus and Serena always had each other to battle. It made them tougher as athletes and, surprisingly, closer as sisters.

That became apparent when the Williams sisters returned to competitive play. As a doubles team, they were practically unstoppable. As singles players, they squared off against each other regularly, trading the number one and number two spots between them. For all those whispering, unpleasant people who said that the Williams sisters offered nothing to the game— well, they got schooled.

Sports critics consider Serena Williams the best female tennis player of all time. She's earned twenty-one grand slam titles and four Olympic gold medals. She's currently the reigning champion of the French Open, the Australian Open, Wimbledon, and the WTA Tour. When Serena isn't ranked number one in the world, Venus usually is. She was the first black American woman to take the number one spot, and has held it three times. She's won seven grand slam titles and her own four Olympic gold medals.

Their path to victory was different from many tennis players, and they've endured hardships other players normally don't but it was obviously the right path for them. As adults, they continue to rule the tennis courts—and they get to share every victory with their best friend: each other.

Tavi Gevinson

Tavi Gevinson
1996–

When she was twelve years old, Tavi Gevinson started a fashion blog called Style Rookie.

Inspired to start her own blog by a friend's older sister, Tavi chose fashion for her subject. She approached fashion like it was an art. It wasn't about what you should wear or a guide on how to be stylish. It was a medium for self-expression. It was a perfect way to share and communicate. Through fashion, Tavi discovered that she could ask questions about herself. Questions like Who am I? and What do I want to be?

Exploring the world of fashion transformed Tavi. Her writing improved, as she was posting in Style Rookie regularly. All through middle school and the beginning of high school, Tavi maintained and curated her blog. At first slowly, then rapidly, her audience grew.

There was no mistaking Tavi's talent and passion.

People found her articles insightful and arresting. She shared a lot of things there. Plenty of style and fashion, and a lot of her own personality, as well. Soon, her blend of confusion and wisdom, uncertainty and boldness, attracted the attention of the fashion establishment. Magazines wrote articles about her. Designers couldn't wait to share their collections with her.

When she was invited to sit at fashion week in New York and Paris, she realized that she wasn't just any kid from Chicago with a blog anymore. Her reputation grew. Her picture appeared in magazines. People followed her style choices. Though she was only fifteen years old, agents clamored for her attention. Traditional fashion magazines courted her.

It was a whirlwind time, but there were also some tough moments. She was no longer under the radar, so people started analyzing Style Rookie. They spread gossip that someone her age couldn't possibly be doing this all on her own. They suspected Tavi's mother or older sister helped her with all the entries. That frustrated her. It implied that teenage girls weren't smart enough or talented enough to earn their own achievements.

She could have been discouraged. She could have

given up. But instead, as a sophomore in high school, she realized this wasn't just about her. There weren't a lot of outlets for teenage girls to talk about being. Just being—being feminist, being afraid, being real, being creative. Most important, there weren't many places where girls' feelings and thoughts were taken seriously.

Through Style Rookie, Tavi had found that place. Now she realized she wanted to create that space for other girls, too.

Tavi set about founding a new magazine, one that didn't try to force girls into a mold. Instead, Tavi's online Rookiemag invited girls to come and be confused and complicated and creative together.

Founded when Tavi was just fifteen, Rookie was a sensation from the moment she announced it. Three thousand people applied to be part of the new magazine's staff. They couldn't wait to be a part of it. When the first issue came out, it was a huge hit.

She has more than three million readers and four published *Rookie Yearbooks*. She doesn't want anyone to think she has all the answers, though. She's still figuring it all out—she's just doing it with three million close, personal friends!

Pelé

Pelé
(Edson Arantes do Nascimento)
1940–

Perhaps Pelé's parents sensed that their firstborn
son had a bright future ahead of him. When he was
born in 1940, they named him after inventor Thomas
Edison.

What Pelé had as a child, however, was a pretty
tough life. The family lived in poverty in Bauru, São
Paulo, in Brazil. To make extra money, Pelé worked as
a servant in local tea shops. Without much money, he
also had to do with makeshift toys. This budding soccer player didn't have fancy equipment. His ball was
a sock stuffed with newspaper—or sometimes an old
grapefruit!

Nimble, with surprising power and confidence,
Pelé proved he didn't need the best of the best to excel. Playing soccer for many youth leagues, he often
led his teams to victory. Starting when he was only

fourteen years old, he and his São Paulo soccer club won the state youth championships three years in a row. And when he wasn't playing outdoor soccer, he could be found playing indoor soccer.

The game was his obsession. Playing both inside and out, he strengthened his game and his stamina. He said that indoor ball taught him to think fast. One of the most important fundamentals in soccer is anticipating where the ball will be, not just understanding where it is. In this way, soccer has a lot in common with chess, and Pelé was turning into a young grandmaster.

His physical prowess was unmatched. All soccer players have to be able to dribble: running while directing the ball between their feet. Pelé went one better and learned how to double dribble. He'd bank the ball off his strong foot with his weak one, sending the ball at an unexpected angle. This signature move made him stand out on the field and often confused his opponents. They just couldn't figure out where the ball would be next when Pelé had it in his possession.

At fifteen years old, Pelé started trying out for professional soccer clubs. In 1956, he signed his very first professional contract with Santos FC. The media swarmed around this gifted young athlete. Everyone was sure he would be the next soccer superstar, and they weren't wrong! Only a few months later, Pelé made his professional debut. Playing against Corinthians Santo André, with Pelé on the pitch, Santos FC won easily. It was an impressive debut!

The very next year, Pelé became a starter for the team. Before the season was out, he'd earn his rank as top scorer in the league. Playing in the World Cup just ten months after signing his first contract, Pelé's debut on the world stage impressed many. Several soccer clubs from around the world tried to woo him. Manchester United and Real Madrid made plays for him.

But not so fast! Brazil was pretty thrilled to have this young champion on their national team. So, to prevent anyone from stealing him away, Brazil declared Pelé a national treasure. So designated, it became illegal to ship him out of the country to play elsewhere! Thus began a forty-year career as one of the finest athletes to ever play soccer.

Ludwig van Beethoven

Ludwig van Beethoven
1770–1827

You've probably already heard of Ludwig van Beethoven. Great composer, went deaf, never gave up his passions. Wrote some of the most magnificent music in the Western world. And all that is true. What you probably haven't heard is what Ludwig accomplished by the age of nineteen.

The thing is, he was not a child prodigy, not really. That was too bad for him, because his dad, Johann, was determined to make him one.

Once a court musician and singer, Johann had the skill to teach music to Ludwig and his siblings. What he didn't have was the ability to teach them well. Instead of gently instructing his children, he terrorized them. Ludwig spent hours at practice, then hours more without dinner if he angered his father during a lesson. Johann beat, starved, and **berated** him.

In spite of that, Ludwig was a good, solid A- student. He had talent and **tenacity**. More important, he loved music. It fascinated him. But his father's erratic training left him undisciplined.

Irritable and frustrated from his father's abuse, Ludwig resisted at every turn. He had started composing, writing his first piece when he was eight, but his home life kept him from blossoming as a composer. The prodigy was in there, but ironically, his father beat it down.

In fact, Johann's plan for getting rich-rich-richer by squeezing every ounce of talent from his kids was a flop. He put them all on display as musical wonders—but they just weren't. Ludwig played just one concert as a child, at the age of eight. Only one, because he wasn't the **wunderkind** Mozart had been. Audiences weren't compelled by a very talented kid at the piano. They wanted an epic genius like Mozart—a hard act to follow.

Finally, the national theater's director saw the potential in Ludwig and took him in as a student. Under careful tutelage, with a teacher who actually cared about his student, Ludwig bloomed. Soon, he was composing sonatas, concertos, and more. Then, he got lessons from the thirty-one-year-old Wolfgang Amadeus Mozart himself.

The best musicians in Europe could clearly see Ludwig's gift. Unlike his father, they coaxed it out instead of beating it down. In fact, Ludwig moved to Vienna to study full time with Mozart for a while. At sixteen, Ludwig had already written enough music to make him a legend. He enjoyed life in Vienna; it was full of music and art. There, he had a family of musicians and friends, people he'd chosen to have in his life.

In fact, Ludwig probably would have stayed there, except his mother fell ill and died. That meant Ludwig's brother and sister were back home, alone with their monster of a father.

Unable to ignore the horrible memories of his own childhood, Ludwig decided he couldn't let his siblings suffer more of the same. After just four months as a student, he went home to Bonn and filed for custody of his siblings. Not only was it granted, the prince granted Ludwig half of his father's wages as child support.

So by the age of nineteen, Ludwig had survived his father's cruel methods. He'd stepped in to save his brother and sister from the same fate. He was a teen dad in a very nontraditional sense, and he was determined to make a better childhood for his siblings than he'd had himself. And he did all of this while writing hundreds of songs, sonatas, and concertos.

Ludwig van Beethoven could have been a child prodigy. Instead, he became a hardworking, determined kid who refused to let his kid sister and brother suffer the way he had. Oh yeah, and then he became a world-famous composer. Even though he lost most of his hearing by the age of twenty-eight, he still managed to write some of the sweetest songs ever written.

That takes more than talent. That takes character, and Ludwig had plenty of that and more.

Gabrielle Turnquest

Gabrielle Turnquest
1995–

If you check out Gabrielle Turnquest's Twitter account (@BabyLitigator), her bio promises that she's not just collecting degrees.

It would be easy to think she might be. First of all, she graduated from high school when she was only thirteen years old. Then she went on to college. For most people, it takes four years to complete a bachelor's degree, but Gabrielle did it in two.

That first degree was in psychology. Even if it were the only one she earned, that would be pretty danged impressive. But Gabrielle comes from a family of lawyers. Her mother and two of her siblings practice law, so she knew a lot about the subject. She knew that an education in law could help her, no matter what she decided to do for a career.

So Gabrielle took advantage of her dual citizenship and moved from the United States to London to attend law school. At sixteen. Two years later, she graduated (most people take three years). Then she sat for the bar exam. This extensive test covers all aspects of the law—and in order to become a practicing lawyer, law students must pass.

In the UK, most law students pass the exam at the age of twenty-seven. Not ambitious Gabrielle. Not only did she sit the exam at the age of eighteen, she aced it. That made her the youngest person in the world to become a lawyer in the United Kingdom!

So if you're counting, so far, that's two degrees in the same amount of time most kids spend getting through high school. Gabrielle wasn't done, though. After conquering the UK bar, she turned around and sat for the bar in the Bahamas. Bam! Third degree, now she was a lawyer in two countries!

Did Gabrielle stop there? Absolutely not! As of this writing, Gabrielle Turnquest is doing what most twenty-year-olds do. She's attending college, as a fashion student. She wants to practice intellectual property and fashion law when she finishes her education.

You know, after she earns her fourth and fifth degrees. No big deal—she's just the girl next door.

She loves pop culture and fashion. If you check out her Twitter account, you'll find it's a gold mine of great stories and links about the fashion industry.

What's interesting is that, according to Gabrielle, anyone could do what she's done. When asked about how she achieved so much in so little time, Gabrielle explained it simply.

"I just had opportunities and programs available to me that I was able to take advantage of."

She's playing down the drive and ambition it took to take advantage of those opportunities. As a young woman on the verge of graduating (again!), it's pretty safe to say that Gabrielle had the opportunities—but more important, she had the vision to see where they could take her.

Making History, Changing the World

In 1907, New York City suffered from a collapsing economy. People made less money, and prices on everything rose, including rent. Landlords hiked rent so high that many people were forced to move out. Then the landlords starting evicting tenants. Why wait for the price to force somebody out? If they just kicked people out, they could rent the apartment to the next people for whatever price they wanted!

Well, sixteen-year-old Pauline Newman decided to do something about it. A Jewish immigrant from Lithuania, Pauline made New York City her home. She worked thirteen hours a day at the Triangle Shirtwaist Factory, but still made time to organize the renters of New York. Coordinating her efforts with other activists, she set a date and set off a rent strike.

Bam! In 1908, Pauline led more than ten thousand families in refusing to pay their rent. They refused to accept **evictions**, too. Now the landlords had apartments stuffed with people who wouldn't leave and wouldn't pay their rent unless the landlords quit overcharging. (And promised not to double or triple the rent in the future as retaliation.)

Biggest rent strike in New York, ever. Finally, the landlords had to give in. This eventually led to rent-control laws and protections for tenants. At only seventeen years old, Pauline Newman had literally changed living conditions for everyone in the city. The newspapers called her the East Side Joan of Arc.

She could have stopped there and secured her place in history, but Pauline didn't like to sit back. The very next year, she helped organize a labor strike to illuminate the horrible conditions that textile workers suffered. This time, forty thousand people went on strike with Pauline. Pretty radical, huh?

Baldwin IV of Jerusalem

Baldwin IV
of Jerusalem
1161–1185

Things haven't changed a whole lot since the twelfth century.

Sure, we have e-readers and they had scrolls, but people are people. Evidence? At the age of nine, tween Prince Baldwin IV of Jerusalem liked to prove he was the coolest kid on the block by offering up his arm. Not for a walk—for torture.

Nobody could hurt him! It didn't matter what they tried, Baldwin could take it. That was the claim. So his friends would take turns. Friction burns? No reaction. Knife pokes? No problem. Fingernail pinches? Bring it on!

They all took turns trying to get a reaction out of him, but Baldwin never flinched. This future king could withstand all kinds of torment without a single hesitation. Did he have a superpower? Well, not exactly.

He had **leprosy**.

No one recognized it at first, because he had no **lesions** yet. His tutor, William of Tyre, figured out the connection when he saw Baldwin IV and his friends taking turns stabbing each other with their fingernails.

Baldwin IV could take the pain because the disease had left his hands and arms numb.

This was pretty bad news for a crown prince. Leprosy would eventually ravage his body. Contrary to popular belief, leprosy doesn't make parts fall off a sufferer's body. In fact, the disease eats away at bone until there's nothing left but flesh. Limbs and digits don't drop away—they shrivel.

There was no way to treat leprosy. Most sufferers died young. But all Baldwin could do was continue his studies and prepare himself to become king. Jerusalem was in the middle of an ongoing war with Saladin, the Sultan of Egypt and Syria. If Baldwin lived long enough to take the throne, it would become his war. He needed to be ready.

And sooner than expected. King Amalric, his father, died of dysentery on the way back from a military campaign. This thrust Baldwin into kingship at the age of thirteen. At first, regents ruled for him. People thought he was too young to actually reign.

(Most suspected he was too sick to reign, too.)

However, two years after his **coronation**, Baldwin took full command of the throne, and the war. His disease had progressed and he needed help to mount his horse, but Baldwin led the battles all the same. At sixteen, he led his army to victory against Saladin at Montisgard. It was a decisive moment, celebrated throughout the empire.

Though an excellent military strategist and a good diplomat, Baldwin was also a realist. He knew he wouldn't live a long life. He wouldn't get the chance to marry—and he wouldn't produce an heir.

After defeating Saladin, Baldwin went back to Jerusalem to make plans for his own death, and for Jerusalem's future. Better safe than sorry, he decided that his nephew, little Baldwin of Montferrat, would become the next king.

When the child was five, he even named him coregent. That meant that Baldwin IV and Baldwin V shared the throne at the same time. But it left no doubt in people's minds who would be the future ruler. This allowed Baldwin IV to make the most of his brief reign.

Not as brief as many expected—Baldwin managed to rule for eleven years. Nevertheless, his death at the age of twenty-four cut short his rule. The invulnerable teen king was mortal, after all.

Kusuo Kitamura

Kusuo Kitamura

1917–1996

Born in Kochi, Japan, Kusuo Kitamura became part of one of the youngest swimming teams in the history of the Olympics.

Swimming had always been a popular sport in Japan. It was considered a military accomplishment in feudal times—a time when many other nations were superstitious about swimming and their citizens refused to learn. Samurai had to learn to swim in full armor; much later, soldiers had to learn to tread water while loading and firing a rifle.

By the early twentieth century, swimming was one of the most popular pastimes in Japan. In a small, island nation, a sport that didn't require huge fields was ideal. Though athletes always tend to skew young, the 1932 Japanese Olympic team was especially so. It was made up entirely of athletes under the age of sixteen.

Among them, Kusuo was the youngest at barely fourteen years old.

He was also the fastest. In the fifteen-hundred-meter freestyle, he swept gold easily—the youngest swimmer in Olympic history to do so. In fact, at the time, he was the youngest person ever to win gold in an Olympic event. (He remains the youngest men's swimmer to do so, a record held for an impressive eighty-three years!)

The 1932 Games were Kusuo's first and last. Despite his amazing success, Kusuo retired from sports after taking gold. He returned to Japan, and to his education. War loomed in the distance, already erupting in Europe. Chances were, Japan would be involved soon, so Kusuo worked hard to graduate from high school before continuing to Tokyo Imperial University.

He wasn't there for long. Just five years after celebrating international sportsmanship at the Olympic Games, Kusuo joined the military to fight in World War II. Materials were scarce during the war. Everyone had to do their part to help. They gave up luxuries and donated treasures they already owned to help the war effort. Kusuo was no different. He donated his gold medal to be melted down, to be used to manufacture machine parts.

The donation touched local authorities. After all, this was the youngest winner in history's gold medal, his only one. Kusuo had retired; there was no chance he could ever win another. The local government couldn't bring themselves to accept the donation. They returned the medal to Kusuo's father so it would be waiting for him after the war.

Kusuo reclaimed it in 1945, after the war ended. He went back to college, to prepare himself for an adult career. And though Kusuo never competed again, he never left swimming behind completely.

The first non-American to be inducted into the International Swimming Hall of Fame, Kusuo continued to support the sport throughout the rest of his life. A member of the Japanese Swimming Federation, he stood sentinel over the next generation of elite Japanese swimmers—secure in the certainty that he knew what it would take to earn gold.

Phillis Wheatley

Phillis Wheatley
c. 1753–1784

No one knew for sure how old Phillis Wheatley was when she was stolen from her family in Senegal or Gambia. Seven or eight was everyone's best guess; after the arduous journey from Africa to Boston, Massachusetts, Phillis was small for her purported age, and sickly at that.

Tailor John Wheatley bought the little girl for his wife, Susannah. She was intended to be a kitchen slave. Whatever her true name, no one asked it. Instead, John Wheatley named her Phillis, after the ship that brought her to the American colonies. Then, as custom, he insisted that she use his last name as her own. This wasn't so much a sign of respect as a mark of ownership.

The newly christened Phillis was old enough to remember her home. Grieving for her lost family, she would spend a few minutes each morning pouring water for the rising sun. This ritual from her homeland was the last vestige of her life before she was kidnapped, and she clung to it for comfort.

The Wheatleys considered themselves kind slave masters. For the time period, they were certainly indulgent. Phillis quickly learned to speak English, which delighted the family. The eldest Wheatley child, Mary, decided to teach Phillis to read and write. This sort of education was rare for white girls in Colonial America, let alone enslaved black girls.

Phillis had a quick and agile mind. Still sickly, she was allowed to spend her time studying instead of working in the kitchen. She represented a novelty—a **literate** enslaved girl—not just able to read and write but with a talent for it. She wrote letters, short stories, and poems.

Years passed, and Phillis turned twelve. She now studied Latin and spent much time translating Ovid's couplets into English.

The Wheatleys couldn't help but brag about Phillis and show her off. They encouraged people to come and talk with her, marveling over her intelligence and conversational skills. Though it was a much gentler enslavement than many other Africans suffered, it was still enslavement. Phillis couldn't choose where to go or what to study; she wasn't free to leave or travel.

This wasn't lost on Phillis, not at all. She sometimes offered subtle critique of her position and treatment in her poems and writings. She couldn't openly
criticize her situation. After all, the people who owned
her could easily sell her or abuse her if she did. The
Wheatleys' friends and family wouldn't be so amused
by an enslaved woman who spoke against them.

Despite the situation, Phillis acclimated to life in
the American colonies. And often wrote fond letters to
members of the Wheatley family. On a trip to New York
with the Wheatley son, she composed a poem for Susannah Wheatley, expressing her homesickness for her.

During this trip, when Phillis was just twenty
years old, she published her first volume of essays
and poems, to great acclaim. The work was so thorough, and so deft, that the leaders of Boston refused
to believe that an enslaved woman could have possibly
written it.

The local church and political elders forced Phillis
to take an exam. During it they quizzed her about her
own book to prove that she had written it. When she
passed the test easily, Phillis's inquisitors had no choice
but to declare her the unquestioned author of *Poems on*

Various Subjects, Religious and Moral.

When Susannah Wheatley died in 1774, John Wheatley finally freed Phillis. For the first time since her kidnapping as a little girl, she belonged to no one but herself. With her newfound liberty, she spent much time corresponding with other artists of color in the Colonies. She found love, as well, in a handsome freedman, John Peters.

As the Revolutionary War began, Phillis continued to write poetry. Unfortunately, still sickly, though no longer a little girl, she suffered a series of losses. Though she and her husband had three children, none of them survived infancy. Lost, too, was Phillis's second volume of poetry, which never found a publisher. Phillis herself passed away when she was only thirty-one years old.

Phillis Wheatley showed remarkable strength and intellect in a time when neither was appreciated or encouraged in people of color. Despite her enslavement, she soaked up all the education afforded her and always reached for more. Aware of her unique position, she tried to encourage other artists of color.

Still, none of us know her true age—and her true name is lost to history.

Salma Kakar

Salma Kakar
1997–

Riding a bicycle shouldn't be controversial. Salma Kakar wants to make it downright ordinary.

This sixteen-year-old girl lives in Afghanistan, where women aren't allowed to drive, and are strongly discouraged from riding bikes. A strict government insists that girls should remain inside whenever possible. And when they go outside? They should be covered from head to toe in a **burqa**.

Salma, however, thinks that girls should have the freedom to ride—and she personally has the goal to make it to the summer Olympics. The lead rider on the Afghan National Cycling Team, Salma and her teammates don't train the way most athletes do. Devout Muslims, they all wear headscarves, long-sleeved shirts, and pants.

And because they're flouting the social roles that

the Taliban and other orthodox groups maintain for women, they often have to practice in the dark. And in secret. They change their practice times and places regularly. To practice out in the open invites certain men to try to interfere. It's happened before. Salma and her teammates have received numerous death threats.

Despite the fact that people literally want to kill her for riding a bike, Salma refuses to give up. All the jeers and obstacles just make her work harder. Many people, including her coach, thought that they might never see girls allowed to ride bikes in their lifetime. With a confident smile, Salma changes that every single day.

Her Olympic dream isn't about winning gold, though she would certainly love to. For Salma, it's about proving that women in Afghanistan are progressing. Already, it's working. People who used to oppose the idea of a women's riding team now support it. Other girls are excited, watching and waiting for the next breakthrough so they can join the fun.

It's easy to wish for change. It's hard to withstand the pressures and the dangers of making it happen. That's why Salma Kakar and her teammates are doing so much more than riding bikes. They're changing their own world, one ride at a time.

Making History, Changing the World

In the late 1800s, newsboys didn't deliver the paper to your house in exchange for a standard wage. They had to buy the newspapers from the publishers—fifty cents for a hundred papers. If they sold all the newspapers, they made a dollar—a profit of fifty cents. Not bad, right?

Well, if they didn't sell all the papers, then they were out of luck. They couldn't return them. They'd already paid for them. Until they sold every last copy, they wouldn't make their full profit. Many newsies would sell late into the night, well past midnight, to make their whole day's wages.

Then publishers hiked the price of a stack of papers to sixty cents. They said it was fair because the newsies were selling more papers on account of the Spanish-American War. Fair enough. However, after the war, two publishers wouldn't drop the price. Now the newsies were earning less and paying more to do their job.

They could have given up. Instead, they fought back with a strike. Refusing to sell their own papers, the newsies shut down the flow of information in New York City. They destroyed papers in the street and encouraged adult workers to join them. They blocked traffic on the Brooklyn Bridge for days, too, to make sure people knew what was happening. (After all, they couldn't read about it in the papers!)

Finally, the publishers gave in. They didn't lower the price of a bundle of papers, but they allowed the newsies to return any papers they hadn't sold for a refund. Now there was no reason for the newsies to suffer late into the night with a few leftover papers to sell. It improved their working conditions immensely and guaranteed each of them a daily profit—a big win for a kids' strike!

Misty Copeland

Misty Copeland
1982–

Most ballet stories start with a young dancer, maybe two or three years old, already at the barre. It's usually a story about a well-off girl who has all the advantages in the world, including private dance teachers, expensive dance gear, and exclusive schools to carve her into a perfect ballerina. Most of the time, this story begins and ends in a glittering, cosmopolitan city like New York, Paris, or Moscow.

Misty Copeland's ballet story started when she was seven, in Bellflower, California. Oh, and it didn't start with ballet—her first love was gymnastics. Not that she took classes; she just loved watching a documentary about a teen gold medalist named Nadia Comaneci. Her family moved to San Pedro, California, a few years later, and Misty fell in love with—wait for it—woodshop class!

She attended that class at the local Boys and Girls Club. Her mother was a medical assistant, and her stepfather a radiologist. They were an average American family, and though Misty loved making up dances to pop music, she didn't get the chance to study ballet until she was thirteen. And was that at an elite ballet academy? Nope. Her first dance experience was in middle school, as part of the drill team.

At thirteen years old, Misty had her very first taste of dance, and she loved it. Not only that, she was good. Her coach recognized Misty's potential to be a great dancer. It just so happened that her coach also knew a ballet teacher at the Boys and Girls Club. Helping Misty make that connection, her coach got her involved in formal training at the club.

At last, Misty had a taste of real dance training! It still wasn't the usual ballerina story. Unlike her competitors, Misty hadn't been training since she could walk. But that's okay—being a prodigy meant she caught up in no time at all.

However, Misty was also a woman of color. Sadly, this led to discrimination that had nothing to do with Misty's ability. Many older ballet instructors and directors want their line of ballerinas to be perfectly uniform in every way—and that included skin color. To them, it didn't matter that Misty was a prodigy, or that she had won the Los Angeles Spotlight Performer Award. What mattered was that she didn't look quite like all the other girls wearing tutus.

Though many people discouraged her from continuing, Misty refused to give up on dancing. For the first time, she felt like she was at home. Dancing was how she expressed herself. When she was on stage, she felt alive. Though competition was fierce, Misty continued to excel. She earned internships at the American Ballet Theatre and was hired to be part of the company in 2001.

As she rose through the ranks of the corps to soloist, she experienced many indignities. Critics called her "too athletic." Even when dance parts were written for her, she was encouraged to use makeup to lighten her skin.

It was humiliating to be treated this way, but Misty was determined. She knew she wasn't the only little girl of color who dreamed about being a dancer. She absolutely would not let discrimination keep her from earning her place in the spotlight.

She wanted to be a role model to other little girls;

she wanted to be onstage and prove that talent was the most important thing. That talent should be the only thing.

Working her way through the ranks of the American Ballet Theatre, Misty danced through injury and setback. She fought through insult and ignorance, becoming first the youngest soloist in the company's history, and the first black soloist in twenty years.

Her story is becoming that happily ever after that gets danced away in *Sleeping Beauty*. After all that hard work and dedication, Misty earned the position of principal dancer in 2015. She's the first black woman to do so in ABT's seventy-five-year history. TIME magazine named her one of 2015's most influential people, and she takes that seriously.

She's said, "You can do anything you want, even if you are being told negative things. Stay strong and find motivation." Part of Misty's journey is paving the way for other young hopefuls like she once was, and she actively works for that. If Misty has her way, she may be the first black principal dancer for ABT, but she definitely won't be the last!

ACTIVIST KIDS!

Not every kid gets to spend their days going to school, playing with friends, and enjoying their family. Some children have to work all day, like Mohammad Manan Ansari did. Manan started working in a mine when he was only eight years old. His shift lasted for nine hours, digging, carrying, and sorting mica—a sharp, brittle mineral used in makeup and electronics.

Manan wasn't the only kid working there in the mine. He said that more than half the young people of Koderma district in Jharkhand, India, worked there. Kids as young as six would put in a full day's work; because of the poverty in their district, families had no choice but to send their young children to work. All this, despite the unsafe working conditions. Most mica has to be dug out of dark, deep pits. Everyone gets cut and scraped, and some unlucky few die when the mining tunnels collapse on them. Manan witnessed his best friend's death during such a collapse, and it continues to haunt him.

When Manan was ten, a local activist group convinced his parents to let Manan go to school instead of to work. Just ten, Manan went first to a rehabilitation academy and then to an actual school near his home. There, he discovered an entirely different world. This one was full of books and learning, sports and good health.

A strong student, Manan worked hard to earn top grades—and now he spends much of his time talking to other families like his. He tells them about the huge difference that education has made in his life. And he encourages parents like his to let their children attend school as well.

With an education, these children have a possibility of a happier, healthier life. Instead of looking forward to decades of hard work in a mica mine, these kids have the chance to become teachers, scientists, artists, and more. Manan is on hand to make sure that as many kids as possible get that chance.

Rosie Casals

Rosemary "Rosie" Casals
1948–

To some, Rosie Casals seemed like an unlikely tennis champ.

The daughter of immigrants from El Salvador, Rosie didn't have the privileges that many young athletes did. She didn't even have the luxuries that most young people did. Money was so tight that her parents realized they couldn't afford to raise Rosie or her sister in San Francisco.

That's when Manuel and Maria Casals—the girls' great-uncle and great-aunt—took them in. They raised the Casals sisters as their very own. Things were better in their great-uncle's house, but they still weren't rich. Having lots of money was often the only way to break into an elite game like tennis.

But not the only way.

There would be no expensive lessons or coaches

for Rosie. Her great-uncle taught her to play tennis on courts in the city parks. Teachers occasionally donated their time and talent. However, Rosie mainly learned from her uncle, who was the only coach she ever had.

And she was good. She could beat just about anybody her age. The unofficial rule that junior players faced off only against other juniors drove her crazy. Rosie wanted to challenge herself. She wanted to play people she wasn't sure she could beat.

That's when she started to enter competitions. Pitting herself directly against older girls gave Rosie the challenge she needed. To be fair, though, Rosie already had a lot of challenges. She wasn't part of the country club set.

She felt very different from the rich kids with their perfectly crisp tennis whites and brand-new shoes. As a Salvadoran, Rosie stood out among her peers anyway. She preferred wearing bright colors* and playing hard, so she stood out even more.

Also? She was tiny, only five feet two—and when she rocked it out on the court, she expected applause. Tennis audiences didn't know how to react to this energetic, unexpected player.

At sixteen, she was the top junior and women's player in California. By seventeen, audiences had learned to appreciate Rosie's gift for the game. As she cruised into eleventh place in world tennis rankings, her fans cheered her on with standing ovations.

Eventually, Rosie teamed up with Billie Jean King. The pair took tennis by storm. They won U.S. titles on clay, grass, indoor, and hard surfaces—the only doubles team ever to achieve that!

Rosie's career continued long after she was a kid. (In fact, she now teaches other kids to play tennis!) It was her extraordinary talent and determination as a kid that gave her that start. She didn't need fancy clothes, tennis shoes, country clubs, or coaches.

All Rosie Casals needed was a racquet and a chance. Her will to compete did the rest!

---

* In fact, Rosie almost got disqualified from Wimbledon because she refused to wear tennis whites!

Quvenzhané Wallis

Quvenzhané Wallis
2003–

When she was just five years old, Quvenzhané (kwuh-VEN-zha-nay) Wallis lied about her age to get into an audition. She wanted to try out for the role of Hushpuppy in a movie called *Beasts of the Southern Wild.* They were only taking actors six years and older, so Quvenzhané took her destiny into her own hands.

She got that audition, and then she bested four thousand other little girls trying out for the part. Though she was completely unknown at the time, Quvenzhané stepped into the role like a pro. Playing the part of a child prodigy, she proved that she was no slouch in that department, either.

Critics loved her, praising her charisma and natural talent on the screen. When the movie premiered at the Sundance Film Festival, it won the Grand Jury Prize. Then six-year-old Quvenzhané got to fly to

France to screen the movie at the internationally esteemed Cannes Film Festival. The movie was touching and raw, a real achievement for any actor.

Though this was her debut as an actor, Quvenzhané turned in a performance so extraordinary that she was nominated for an Academy Award for Best Actress. Though she didn't win (that honor went to twenty-two-year-old Jennifer Lawrence), to be nominated for an Oscar at all is impressive; check out how many first-evers she racked up at the same time:

* First African American child actor to be nominated for an Oscar.
* First nominee born in the twenty-first century.
* Youngest Best Actress nominee ever.
* Third youngest nominee overall.*

If you think Quvenzhané is done as an actor, you're dead wrong. She's already starred in five more movies, including the modern-day retelling of the musical *Annie.* This young actor has a long career ahead of her, and what's more, she has some special talents to help her along the way.

The director of *Beasts of the Southern Wild* actually changed the script for Quvenzhané. He wanted to include her incredible personality, her ear-piercing scream, and her ability to burp on command!

* The other two are Justin Henry, who was eight when he filmed *Kramer vs. Kramer,* and Tatum O'Neal, who was ten years old when she won for her performance in 1973's *Paper Moon.*

Helen Keller

Helen Keller
1880–1968

Born in Tuscumbia, Alabama, Helen Keller was her parents' first child together. (She had two grown stepbrothers, from her father's first marriage.)

Everyone doted on Helen. Wild and full of energy, Helen ran her family ragged with her exuberance. They called her Little Bronco—not the chillest kid in the world, for sure!

She fell ill at nineteen months old. Raging with a high fever, she clung to her mother for days. Then suddenly, the fever disappeared. Helen was well again—except, the world was so quiet and dark to her, it felt like nighttime all the time.

It took her parents a while to realize that the fever had left Helen both deaf and blind. The Kellers' friends and family encouraged them to put Helen in an **institution**. That was the most common way of dealing with people with disabilities in the nineteenth century.

They didn't think people with disabilities could do very much, and many thought that it was too much of a burden for the family to care for them. At least in an institution, they would have people to look after them. They wouldn't end up homeless or alone.

Nevertheless, the Kellers refused. Yes, Helen was deaf and blind, but she was still their Little Bronco. They didn't want to send her away. They knew she wouldn't get an education in the institution. She would stay with her family, and they would hire a teacher for her.

By using her sense of touch, Helen could handle doing chores. She recognized her family's clothes by touch, and she had the responsibility of folding them. However, don't get the impression that Helen was a perfect little angel. Hardly!

When the Kellers' cook brought her daughter to the house, she and Helen would play together.

Once, they started out cutting bits of ribbon and paper with scissors. They moved on to their clothes, and then their hair! Another time, they **absconded** with a freshly baked cake and ate it in secret in the garden.

Things could be hard, too. Often angry and frustrated, Helen would throw tantrums when she couldn't get her point across. She invented her own form of sign language. To ask for her father, she pretended to put on his glasses. Her sign for mother was a hand on her cheek. Hungry? Well, for bread, Helen pretended to cut and butter a loaf. For ice cream, she shivered.

These signs, however sophisticated, were limited. Of course Helen understood them, and sometimes her parents did, too. But Helen had no way to express how she was feeling.

By the time Helen was seven, she keenly felt the gulf between herself and her family. They didn't understand her, and she couldn't make herself understood. Later, she would call this time in her life the "no-world." Though she had plenty of ideas, thoughts, and feelings, she had no way to share them.

No way, that is, until the Kellers hired a woman named Anne Sullivan to come help her. Sullivan was also visually impaired, and she had attended the Perkins School for the Blind. When she was young, Sullivan had been a little bronco, too. Her teachers called her Miss Spitfire.

So when Helen and Sullivan met, they clashed. Helen didn't know what Sullivan wanted, and Sullivan wasn't sure how to teach her. Eventually, though, they figured it out.

Sullivan spelled words into Helen's hand, but Helen didn't realize what they meant. It was just a game; to her, milk and mug meant the same thing. One day, Sullivan took Helen to the water pump outside. Holding Helen's hand under the spout, she spelled water into her palm. Then she pumped cold, clean water onto Helen's hand.

Water. Water! That wet stuff, that stuff she could drink, it was water, and mug was the vessel that held it! It was the moment she connected Sullivan's finger spelling with words. With communication!

This, Helen said later, was her soul's birthday.

Suddenly, she had gone from her no-world, and had entered a place where she could share her thoughts and feelings. She was no longer alone.

Helen soaked up everything. Soon, she could read several **embossed** alphabets, including braille. Learning to write, she could create braille texts with a **stylus**, and she could also write in standard print with a pencil or pen.

Helen became a prolific letter writer, and reader. And hey, since she was learning to speak anyway, she asked to learn French. And Greek. (Eventually, she also learned German and Latin!)

Once she had a chance to learn, Helen refused to stop. At eight years old, she and Sullivan went to the Perkins School for the Blind. For the first time, Helen learned mathematics, history, science, and more.

But Helen wouldn't slow down. She'd spent a lot of time alone, before she could read, write, even have a conversation. Now, the Little Bronco would make it up and then some!

Helen Keller had always been smart (and lively!). But she was also lucky to have parents who had the resources to insist on her education. Even luckier still, she found a teacher in Anne Sullivan, and a lifelong friend as well.

Helen went on to attend high school, and then college (she was the first deaf and blind woman to earn her bachelor's degree in the United States). Then, she spent the rest of her life helping other people with disabilities.

She knew how much she had accomplished, and how much others like her had to offer. Institutionalization had seemed like a kind idea at the time, but Helen knew better. Giving people with disabilities an equal chance to learn, grow, and work was the right way.

She never stopped sharing that message during her lifetime—and beyond. Through her books and letters, she still shares that message today.

Louis Braille

Louis Braille

1809–1852

Louis Braille was born sickly, but not visually impaired. He was the baby of the Braille family, spoiled and adored by everyone who knew him.

When he was three, he invited himself to play in his father's workshop. The Brailles made tack for horses—saddles, reins, bridles. Louis settled in to work with his father, toying with a bit of leftover leather.

Historians disagree on what happened next. Some say that Louis tried to cut the leather with a scalpel. Others say he tried to punch holes in it with an **awl**.

In any case, the tool skated off the leather and injured Louis's eye. The Brailles rushed Louis to the best surgeon they could find. Unfortunately, there was little the surgeon could do but bandage him. An infection raged through the wound, which spread to

Louis's other eye. By the time he turned five, he was completely blind.

Louis was always his parents' favorite. They knew he was smart, and they insisted that he be allowed to attend school with all the other children in the village of Coupvray, France, where they lived. It was seriously rare for someone with visual impairments to get an education at all. The Brailles insisted that Louis get the best.

Until he was ten, Louis studied at the village school. Then a family friend wrote to the Royal Institute for Blind Youth to tell them about this inquisitive, creative boy. That recommendation earned Louis a place in one of the very first schools for the visually impaired.

The Royal Institute (which became the National Institute after the French Revolution) aspired to give visually impaired children a complete education, and hopefully vocational training. The impediment was literacy—how do you teach the visually impaired to read and write?

Writing was slightly less tricky. They memorized the shapes of letters by tracing a **stylus** in a board carved with each letter shape. Each student had a wire board to lay over paper. Using pencils, the students carefully plotted out each letter. The wires kept them from straying into other lines.

Compared to writing, reading was tricky. The best technology at the time was **embossed** books. Instead of printing with ink, publishers pressed the letter shapes into wet paper. Then they sewed these pages front to back and bound them. A single book could weigh eighteen pounds or more!

Louis read these embossed books over and over, even though it was tough. Still, he longed to read more. Around that time, a military code maker created a tactile alphabet and convinced the school to let him test it on its students.

This system was made up of long series of dots. It was originally designed to send military messages that could be read in the dark. It was even called night writing! It seemed like the perfect solution for visually impaired literacy.

Unfortunately, this code was incredibly difficult to memorize. There was a six-by-six grid, broken down by the sounds of words instead of by letters. Though this method worked slightly better than embossing, Louis thought there had to be an easier way.

Rather than wait for someone else to invent it, Louis got to work himself. He knew how hard it was to make out curved, embossed shapes—and how unwieldy embossed books could be. He also knew that the night writing dots were easier, but not easy. There was too much to memorize. It relied on people pronouncing words exactly the same way.

So Louis mulled over the problem. By twelve, he had started building his new raised alphabet. As he did, he had specific needs in mind. He wanted each letter to fit underneath a fingertip. It was important for children to be able to understand the rules. Finally, it needed to reflect the language as it was written, not spoken.

Devising a six-cell method, Louis tested and edited and refined his new script. Teaching it to his fellow students at the institute, he made changes to make it easier to learn. Their feedback was invaluable. They, too, knew what it was like to be blind; they also knew what they needed to be **literate**.

At sixteen, Louis published his new alphabet. It was wildly successful. It gave its readers a way to finally jot down notes for later, rather than relying entirely on memory. They could write letters without the help of scribes or wire boards, and read books without assistance.

Because he had such a full education, Louis Braille was able to support himself as a musician for most of his life. But his first passion was his alphabet. He spent most of his time perfecting it. Today, we still use braille. It's changed very little since the nineteenth century.

If Louis's parents hadn't insisted on accommodations for their son, if the schools had refused to educate this bright young man, he never would have had the chance to invent exactly the alphabet that he and the visually impaired world needed.

Indeed, it would be a much smaller world for everyone.

How to Read Braille

Compared to other raised-letter systems, Louis Braille's was a masterpiece of simplicity.

He assigned a six-dot unit for each character. But instead of memorizing fifty-two different letters (upper and lower case, and then in French, all the accents!) the reader memorizes ten letter positions. Here are the first ten.

a	b	c	d	e	f	g	h	i	j

The first row shows you where on the cell grid that the dots are arranged. The second row shows you braille without guides (this is how it appears in books for the visually impaired).

Now, to learn the next ten. Louis could have started over with all new shapes. Instead, he added a dotted cell to the previous ten. This dot told readers that they were in the middle of the alphabet now.

k	l	m	n	o	p	q	r	s	t

The top four cells remain the same; the only change is the addition of a cell in the lower left of each character.

On to the final six letters. In French, there's no native W. The only time they use it is for writing foreign words—usually names. This is the one place that braille deviates slightly from its own formula. Since X already sat where W should have been, Louis added W to the end of the alphabet.

u   v   x   y   z   w

Now, the only thing that changes is the addition of a dotted cell in the lower right of each character.

In Louis's original grid, there are a few more rows following the same pattern, to create all the accented letters needed. Since you don't need a ç or an à in English, we skipped those.

Finally, some punctuation.

,   ?   -   .   !   '   CAP

Punctuation takes all new cell forms. This way, they cannot be mistaken for letters. To create a capital letter, the CAP sign is added in front of the letter to modify.

Once you know how braille works, it's easy to learn to read it. Louis designed it to be easy. It's legible by sight and by touch, to the very young and the very old.

Since you just had your first lesson, you need to practice. Check out the jokes and trivia written in braille on the next few pages and see if you can decipher their meaning.

Here's one to get you started:

Did you figure it out? It says, "Scrabble was invented by a guy named Alfred Mosher Butts!" (And it was!)

Braille

JOKES

1. [Braille text]

2. [Braille text]

3. [Braille text]

4. [Braille text]

5. [Braille text]

6. [Braille text]

See page 284 for the answer key!

Braille

TRIVIA

1. ⠨⠁⠇⠁⠎⠅⠁ ⠊⠎ ⠮ ⠍⠕⠎⠞ ⠝⠕⠗⠮⠗⠝⠄ ⠺⠑⠎⠞⠻⠝ ⠁⠝⠙ ⠑⠁⠎⠞⠻⠝ ⠎⠞⠁⠞⠑ ⠊⠝ ⠮ ⠠⠥⠄⠠⠎⠄

2. ⠨⠊⠎⠗⠁⠑⠇ ⠊⠎ ⠮ ⠕⠝⠇⠽ ⠉⠳⠝⠞⠗⠽ ⠊⠝ ⠮ ⠨⠍⠊⠙⠙⠇⠑ ⠠⠑⠁⠎⠞ ⠺⠊⠹⠳⠞ ⠁ ⠙⠑⠎⠻⠞⠲

3. ⠠⠮ ⠕⠝⠇⠽ ⠋⠊⠎⠓ ⠹⠁⠞ ⠉⠁⠝ ⠃⠇⠊⠝⠅ ⠺⠊⠹ ⠃⠕⠹ ⠑⠽⠑⠎ ⠊⠎ ⠁ ⠎⠓⠁⠗⠅⠲

4. ⠠⠽⠳⠗ ⠞⠕⠝⠛⠥⠑⠏⠗⠊⠝⠞ ⠊⠎ ⠚⠥⠎⠞ ⠁⠎ ⠥⠝⠊⠟⠥⠑ ⠁⠎ ⠽⠳⠗ ⠋⠊⠝⠛⠻⠏⠗⠊⠝⠞⠎

5. ⠠⠺⠊⠹⠳⠞ ⠁ ⠞⠊⠍⠽ ⠺⠁⠎⠏ ⠋⠗⠥⠊⠞ ⠋⠇⠊⠑⠎ ⠝⠑⠧⠻ ⠙⠑⠧⠑⠇⠕⠏ ⠁ ⠺⠁⠎⠞⠲

6. ⠠⠮ ⠎⠉⠊⠑⠝⠞⠊⠋⠊⠉ ⠞⠻⠍ ⠋⠕⠗ ⠮ ⠠⠇⠕⠉⠓ ⠠⠝⠑⠎⠎ ⠠⠍⠕⠝⠎⠞⠻ ⠊⠎ ⠠⠝⠑⠎⠎⠊⠞⠻⠁⠎ ⠗⠓⠕⠍⠃⠕⠏⠞⠻⠽⠭⠲

See page 284 for the answer key!

Which Epic Kid
Are You?

Have you ever wanted to meet your match? As in, your famous kid personality match, of course! Take this quick quiz to find out which epic kid could be your best friend!

1. In the middle of your spelling test, you notice one of your classmates trying to copy off you. You . . .

A) Cover your paper, then discreetly point this out to your teacher after class. What they're doing isn't right, and they need to know that.

B) Consider the possibilities. Maybe their dog died and they didn't have a chance to study. Or maybe they're cheating themselves out of their own education. This is a good chance for you to think about what you would do if you were in their position.

C) Don't really care. If they want to cheat themselves out of their own education, let them. More power for you!

D) Consider all the possibilities. Why is that student cheating? What makes it easy to do so? What would make it harder? There's got to be a great solution to this problem; you just have to figure it out.

E) Catch their eye and give them a warning look. If they peep again, nail them with your fastest spitball. It's an easy shot from here!

2. Your parents agree to take you and your siblings out for the day. The only catch is, you all have to agree on the destination. You . . .

A) Explain why your selection would be the right choice, and refuse to back down. When you're right, you're right.

B) Get everyone to put their ideas into a hat. Then each of you pick an idea and argue for it—even if it's not yours. Debate is good for you!

C) There will be no discussion. It's your way or the highway—everybody else can just deal with it!

D) Create a list of things you want out of an outing, and have your siblings do it, too. Now, using those lists, choose a destination based on everyone's desires.

E) You're flexible. You love all kinds of stuff, and you know there will be other chances to choose in the future.

3. The best word to describe you is . . .

A) Principled.

B) Thoughtful.

C) Divine.

D) Innovative.

E) Confident.

4. Somebody is messing around with a littler kid at the bus stop. You . . .

A) Step in and make sure that the littler kid is safe, and refuse to back down until he is. People have to take a stand for human rights.

B) Whittle the bully down to size with a subtle and sarcastic flurry of wordplay.

C) It's not your job to protect that kid. He needs to learn to stand up for himself.

D) Figure out how to defuse the situation. There must be a solution that works for everyone and makes the bus stop a better place.

E) Block the bully and tell him to go pick on someone his own size. You're not afraid of a little defense.

5. You and a friend were supposed to do a book report together. It's due tomorrow, and only your half is complete. You . . .

A) Deliver your half of the report with confidence. The teacher can't hold you responsible for someone else's bad judgment. (And if she does, you can always appeal to the principal.)

B) Write the other half, from the perspective of a tiny ang-
lerfish. It's a creative choice (and your friend can't com-
plain, since she didn't make any choices of her own!)

C) Are perfectly happy to do the fun parts of the project.
If the rest doesn't get finished, oh well. It's not your
problem

D) Encourage your best friend to finish her half of the report, even if it is last minute. It may not be perfect, but
you'll both get more out of the experience if you try to
complete it together.

E) Call foul. That's really bad sportsmanship.

6. If you could volunteer for any cause, what would it be?

A) Civil rights.

B) Women's rights.

C) Your own right to tell everybody what to do.

D) Protecting the environment.

E) Equal opportunity for all.

Count up your answers. If you have 4 of any single letter, that's your kid twin! If you have 3/3, then you're a
split decision. If you have a little bit here or there, then
consider all the final choices. There's a little bit of you in
each one!

MOSTLY A: You're strong, you're not wrong, and you're ready to stand up for your rights—just like Claudette Colvin (p. 64)! You know it might be hard to do the right thing sometimes, but the result is always worth it!

MOSTLY B: You don't have all the answers, and you don't pretend you do—just like Tavi Gevinson (p. 206). The important thing is that you're always ready to question yourself and your beliefs. That means the ones that stick are really important to you.

MOSTLY C: Hate to break it to you, but you and Elagabalus (p. 194) are >>like this<<. It's tons of fun to be the villain. Just don't forget that another thing you have in common with this teen Roman emperor is the possibility that everybody's plotting against you.

MOSTLY D: Changing the world is your game, just like Param Jaggi (p. 8). You both know that you don't have to be an adult or a millionaire (or both) to start making your community a better place.

MOSTLY E: Nice! Nobody gets one past you, just like your twin on the mound, Mo'ne Davis (p. 44)! You know exactly what you're good at, and you're confident that you can work hard to become even better.

SPLIT DECISION: Kim Ung-yong (p. 56) is you all over! No matter what other people think, you know that the pursuit of happiness is the meaning of life!

Braille answer key

JOKES:

1. Why was six afraid of seven? Because seven eight nine!

2. Why couldn't the bike stand on its own? It was two tired!

3. What's red and bad for your teeth? A brick.

4. What do you call a beat boxing dinosaur? A velocirapper!

5. What do cats eat for breakfast? Mice crispies!

6. What does a snail say on a turtle's back? Wheee!

TRIVIA:

1. Alaska is the most northern, western and eastern state in the USA.

2. Lebanon is the only country in the Middle East without a desert.

3. The only fish that can blink with both eyes is a shark.

4. Your tongueprint is just as unique as your fingerprint!

5. Without a tinman gene, fruit flies never develop a heart.

6. The scientific name for the Loch Ness Monster is Nessiteras rhombopteryx.

Vocabulary Guide

to abscond—to steal, to take off with. (In 1932, a mysterious stranger absconded with famous pilot Charles Lindbergh's son in the middle of the night.)

to assassinate—to commit a politically motivated murder; usually the killing of a prominent political or social leader. (Gavrilo Princip was only twenty when he assassinated Austrian Archduke Ferdinand and touched off World War I.)

awl—a small, pointed tool, usually used to poke holes in leather, wood, metal, or paper. (Before the invention of the lasting machine in 1883, kids worked in factories, using a peg and an awl to make shoes by hand.)

ballistics—using geometry and physics to study and understand the path taken by a projectile. (Studying ballistics is a good way to learn to be a better soccer player. Or, you could emulate Pelé, considering he's one of the best!)

to berate—to criticize someone; to talk to someone angrily. (When Zach Wahls was nineteen, he berated Iowa lawmakers for trying to pass a law against marriage equality; his speech went viral on the Internet.)

to broker—to help two or more parties reach an agreement. (Deliberately and with careful diplomacy, Pocahontas brokered an eight-year peace between her people and the European settlers.)

burqa—a full-length gown with a veil and head-covering, worn by some Muslim women. (To protest the banning of burqas in France, teenage girls from many religions wore burqas in solidarity with their Muslim friends.)

centrifuge—a scientific machine that spins materials at high speed, usually to separate the contents. (At the age of fifteen, Jack Andraka learned to use a centrifuge to detect proteins; he put knowledge together with carbon nanotubes and blot paper—inventing a pancreatic cancer detection test that costs only three cents per test.)

civil engineering—the field of study that concerns itself with maintaining and expanding various living environments. It's especially focused on engineered civilization like roads, bridges, tunnels, and more. (In Japan, civil engineers have to take earthquakes, tsunamis, and population density into consideration when they plan a structure. They do not, however, worry about giant lizard invasions.)

confederation—a group of like-minded people who join together to achieve a specific goal. (Based in Algiers, the Pan African Youth Movement is an international confederation that rallies kids to fight for African freedom.)

contemplation—deep, considered thought about a

particular subject. (Even though she was a mathematical genius, Maria Agnesi preferred to spend her time in religious contemplation.)

coronation—the crowning of a monarch. (Isabella II of Spain technically became queen at the age of three, but she didn't have her coronation until she was thirteen.)

cubism—a style of art that condenses an image into geometric shapes, trying to capture the essence of a scene rather than record it as it existed. (Born in 1999, teen cubist painter Hamad Al Humaidhan, known as Hamadi, is considered the world's next Pablo Picasso.)

to dissent—to publicly disagree with a given position; usually used when referring to opposing the law or the government. (There are lots of ways to dissent—twenty-one-year-old Emma Sulkowicz protested her university's response to sexual assault at the school by carrying her mattress everywhere on campus.)

dissertation—an in-depth, written report of research that expands and extends someone's field of study. (Graduate students must write a dissertation to earn their PhD.)

embossed—figures, shapes, or letters pressed into a surface to create a raised impression. (When teen king Edward VI wrote his Devise for Succession, he embossed it with his official seal.)

to emulate—to copy; to act like. (Some people accuse Lady Gaga of doing her best to emulate Madonna. Of course, during the height of Madonna's popularity, people accused Madonna of trying to emulate actress Marilyn Monroe.)

to evict—to force someone out of a building or a position; usually used to describe forcing people out of their homes. (Conditions have to be pretty bad for tenants to consider a rent strike. If they don't get enough support, landlords can simply evict them.)

gambit—an untried attempt to make a specific outcome happen. (Experimental plays in a game of chess are often called gambits—their outcome isn't guaranteed, but the attempt is worth the risk.)

ghetto—low-quality housing, usually inhabited by poor or forcibly relocated people. (In the United States, ghetto usually refers to low-income housing; in Europe, it usually refers to places where governments force certain people to live.)

heretic—someone who speaks or acts against the laws of a particular religion. (Eight-year-old pharaoh Tutankhamun restored all the Egyptian gods to places of honor, just a few years after his heretic father had declared them nonexistent.)

hydraulic (system)—a system that uses liquids to control and direct mechanical parts. (At eighteen years old, Blaise Pascal invented the calculator. A few years later, when he was just twenty-four, he invented the syringe and the hydraulic press.)

hysterectomy—a surgery to remove a woman's diseased or damaged uterus. (The first hysterectomy was performed in 1843. It wasn't until 1853, however, that a patient actually survived the surgery.)

indigenous—the people native to a region, before foreign expansion or colonialization. (Indigenous children in North America often earned a new name based on their accomplishments. At the age of fourteen, a boy named Jumping Badger earned the name Tatanka Iyotake following a horse raid against the neighboring Crow. You know him better as Sitting Bull.)

to institutionalize—to put someone into the permanent care of a government or medical ward, in theory for their own well-being and protection. (In the late 1800s, teenage girls were often institutionalized for "moral crimes"—for example, going out on a date without a chaperone!)

laparoscopic—a surgery technique that uses a lighted camera to look inside the abdomen, allowing surgeons to operate with very small incisions. (Some doctors compare laparoscopic surgery to playing video games, especially when they use a robot to do the stitching.)

leprosy—a bacterial disease that causes skin lesions, muscle weakness, nerve damage, and destruction of bone. (People think that leprosy makes body parts fall off—this isn't true. What it does is destroy small bones like fingertips, making the fingers appear to shrink or disappear.)

lesion—damage on the skin caused by illness or injury. (If you bottle-feed lambs or play in pastures, watch out for dark reddish-blue lesions on your fingers or hands; you might have caught a pox virus called orf.)

literate—knowing how to read and write. (Poet Phillis Wheatley was literate at a time when it was illegal in the United States for enslaved people to read or write.)

lynching—A public execution by a mob; most often used to refer to the hangings and burnings of African Americans in the United States by large groups of white Americans during the 19th and 20th Centuries. (Lynchings claimed more than three thousand lives in the United States between 1882 and 1930.)

nanoparticle—a very, very, very, extremely teensy-weensy object that acts like it's a unit all by itself. (Even though nanoparticles are smaller than the width of a human hair, they can be used to create frost-free windows, graffiti-resistant paint, drug delivery methods, and DNA probes.)

neutrino—particles created by the decay of radioactive elements, lacking an electrical charge. (The word *neutrino* comes from Italian, meaning "little neutral one." Check that out: dictionary inception. A definition in a definition!)

orator—a speaker; one who gives speeches. (Sumedha Mangesh Trifaley is the youngest orator in India's history; she gave her first speech at the age of four, to an audience of thousands.)

photosynthesis—the process of converting light into energy; usually refers to the way plants use sunlight for food. (*Rhizanthella gardneri* is an orchid that lives entirely underground—it's one of the few plants in the world that doesn't use photosynthesis to feed itself!)

polygamy—a marriage of one man and multiple women. There is also polyandry, a marriage of one woman and many men. (Though the Romans are famous for all kinds of vices, polygamy wasn't one of them. Not even their gods were allowed to have more than one spouse!)

prototype—the original model of an invention; sometimes functional, sometimes not. (An engineer named Lonnie Johnson was supposed to be inventing a better fridge. Instead, he accidentally invented a prototype for the Super Soaker water gun!)

pseudonym—a false name; a name that someone uses in place of their real one. (When Charlotte, Emily, and Anne Brontë started publishing, they used male pseudonyms: Currer, Ellis, and Acton Bell.)

rhetoric—the art of using language effectively and powerfully, usually in speeches or persuasive writings. (The kids who participate in the Young Orators competitions have to brush up on their rhetoric if they want to win.)

satire—the use of humor, exaggeration, and mockery to criticize something or someone. (Jonathan Swift wrote a satire encouraging the Irish to eat their own children, as a solution to the hardships they suffered under British landowners.)

skirmish—a small, insignificant fight that usually precedes a major battle. (In 1895, *The New York Times* ran a story claiming that everyone in Jackson Hole, Wyoming, had died in a massacre. Actually, there had been a minor skirmish over a piece of land; only two people died.)

sovereign—a supreme ruler, usually a king/queen or emperor/empress. (At the age of two, Aisin-Gioro Puyi became the last emperor of China; as a sovereign, he abdicated his position when he was just six.)

stylus—a wand or stick used to make marks; for example, in clay, on wax, on your iPad. (In ancient Rome, students completed their schoolwork by writing on a wax tablet with a stylus.)

to suture—to bring together; usually referring to the use of medical instruments to close a wound. (You don't need thread or staples to suture a wound—ancient people throughout the world encouraged large ants to bite wounds closed, then popped off their heads to leave the living stitches in place.)

tactile—relating to the sense of touch; or being a very touchy-feely person. (Babies are very tactile. Their eyesight isn't very good, and they don't yet speak a language, but they can touch things to learn more about their world.)

tenacity—having the determination to stick to something, or to see something through. (It took one new driver in South Korea 960 tries and a lot of tenacity to pass the country's driving test.)

timbre—a unique, distinct quality in tone—usually used

to describe music or art; sometimes used to describe a mood or feeling. (Though Stevie Wonder plays the piano like a boss, the way he plays a harmonica gives his compositions their timbre.)

treatise—a scholarly paper that systematically examines a subject in great depth. (If you even sort of mention apparating in Hogwarts, Hermione Granger will write you a treatise on why it's not possible.)

typhus—an infectious disease characterized by high fever, rashes, back pain, headaches, and, very frequently, death. (Frank Robert Pierce, the son of the fourteenth president of the United States, died of typhus at the age of four.)

vagabond—a wanderer, someone who moves from place to place without settling down. (Many Swingkinder during World War II were accused of being vagabonds. Charged with the crime of *arbeitsscheu* (work shyness), they were often exiled to concentration camps.)

wunderkind—German for wonder kid—a prodigy. (Mozart was a musical wunderkind; he wrote his first compositions at the age of five!)

Bibliography

"A Child Worker's Journey—from Jharkhand to Geneva." *The Times of India*, n.d. Web. 21 May 2015.

Adams, Simon. Alexander: *The Boy Soldier Who Conquered the World*. Washington, D.C.: National Geographic Society, 2005. Print.

Adler, David A., John Wallner, and Alexandra Wallner. *A Picture Book of Louis Braille*. New York: Holiday House, 1997. Print.

"Alexander the Great (Alexander of Macedon) Biography." *History of Macedonia*.Org. History of Macedonia, n.d. Web. 14 Dec. 2014.

Appiah, Anthony, and Henry Louis Gates. *Africana: The Encyclopedia of the African and African American Experience: The Concise Desk Reference*. Philadelphia: Running, 2003. Print.

Bayne-Powell, Rosamond. *The English Child in the Eighteenth Century*. New York: E. P. Dutton and Company, 1939. Print.

Bodo, Peter, and David Hirshey, with Pelé. *Pelé's New World*. New York: W. W. Norton Company, 1977. Print.

Bondy, Katie. "Growing Up 18th Century Style." *Eighteenth Century England*. University of Michigan, n.d. Web. 13 Dec. 2014.

Boyd, Duke, and Jeff Divine. *Legends of Surfing*. Minneapolis: MVP Books, 2009. Print.

Bradley, Michael. *Benchmark All Stars: Serena Williams*. Tarrytown, NY: Benchmark Books, 1962. Print.

Brimner, Larry Dane. *Pocahontas: Bridging Two Worlds*. Tarrytown, NY: Marshall Cavendish Benchmark, 2009. Print.

Brown Marsh, Marion. *Sacagawea: Indian Interpreter to Lewis and Clark*. Chicago: Childrens Press, 1988. Print.

Butterfield, Bonnie. "What Happened After the Expedition:

Sacagawea's Death." *Native Americans: The True Story of Sacagawea and Her People.* Bonnie Butterfield, n.d. Web. 17 Feb. 2015.

Cavazzi, Franco. "Elagabalus." *The Illustrated History of the Roman Empire.* Roman-Empire.Net, n.d. Web. 19 Feb. 2015.

"Child Miners: The Dig for Freedom." *MTV Voices.* MTV, 17 Nov. 2014. Web. 21 May 2015.

Chin-Lee, Cynthia, Megan Halsey, and Sean Addy. *Amelia to Zora: Twenty-six Women Who Changed the World.* Watertown, MA: Charlesbridge, 2005. Print.

Chmielewski, Dawn. "Teen Phenom Tavi Gevinson Talks About Her Magazine, Fashion Blog—and Finishing High School (Video)." *Recode. Re/Code,* 18 Feb. 2015. Web. 21 Feb. 2015.

"Circa June 1748: Publication of Analytical Institutions." *This Month in Physics History.* American Physical Society, 01 June 2010. Web. 13 Dec. 2014.

Clark, Meredith. "9-year-old Activist Saves Chicago School, Dreams Big." *MSNBC.com.* NBC News Digital, 12 Sept. 2013. Web. 21 May 2015.

Conner, Floyd. *Olympics' Most Wanted: The Top 10 Book of Gold Medal Gaffes, Improbable Triumphs, and Other Oddities.* Washington, D.C.: Brassey's, 2001. Print.

Cooney, Kara. *The Woman Who Would Be King.* New York: Crown, 2014. Print.

Cooney, Miriam P., editor. *Celebrating Women in Mathematics and Science.* Reston, VA: National Council of Teachers of Mathematics, 1996. Print.

Cooper, Dan. *Enrico Fermi and the Revolution of Modern Physics.* New York: Oxford University Press, 1999. Print.

Copeland, Misty, and Charisse Jones. *Life in Motion: An Unlikely Ballerina.* New York: Touchstone, 2014. Print.

Copeland, Misty, and Christopher Myers. *Firebird.* New York: G. P. Putnam's Sons, 2014. Print.

Corder, Mike. "History: Anne Frank Died 1 Month Earlier

Than Previously Thought, Museum Says." *Time Magazine*;
Time Inc. 31 March 2015. Print.

Crowe, Ellie, and Illustrations by Richard Waldrep. *Surfer of
the Century: The Life of Duke Kahanamoku*. New York: Lee &
Low Books, 2007. Print.

Donaldson, Madeline. *Venus & Serena Williams*: Revised Edi-
tion. Minneapolis: Lerner Publishing Group, 2008. Print.

Douglas, Gabrielle, and Michelle Burford. *Grace, Glory &
Gold: My Leap of Faith*. Grand Rapids: Zondervan, 2012.
Print.

Duggan, Johnny. "10 Kid Activists Who Will Make You Feel
Lazy." *RYOT News*. RYOT Corporation, 20 Jan. 2014.
Web. 12 Dec. 2014.

Duke Kahanamoku. *Big Island Television*, 2009. Web.

"Duke Kahanamoku Biography—A Hawaiian Childhood,
Olympic Star, Chronology, Awards and Accomplishments,
the Father of Surfing." *Sports JRank*. Net Industries, n.d.
Web. 21 Feb. 2015.

"Duke Kanahamoku—Hawaii's Greatest Athlete." *Aloha Hawaii RSS*. Aloha from Hawaii, n.d. Web. 21 Feb. 2015.

Edelman, Cris. "Maria Gaetana Agnesi." *History of Mathematics for Middle School Teachers*. Wichita State University Department of Mathematics and Statistics, n.d. Web.
12 Dec. 2014.

Edmondson, Jacqueline. *Venus and Serena Williams: A Biography*. Westport, CT: Greenwood Press, 2005. Print.

"FAMU Freshman Continues to Excel After Inventing Surgical Technique at Age 14." *News Headlines*. Florida A&M
University, 29 Nov. 2012. Web. 21 Feb. 2015.

Ford, Carin T., Helen Keller: *Lighting the Way for the Blind
and the Deaf*. Berkeley Heights, NJ: Enslow Publishers,
2001.

Foreman, Laura. *Alexander the Conqueror: The Epic Story of the
Warrior King*. Cambridge, MA: Da Capo, 2004. Print.

Gay, Roxane. *Bad Feminist: Essays*. New York: HarperPeren-
nial, 2014. Print.

Gevinson, Tavi. "A Teen Just Trying to Figure It Out." *TEDx-Teen*. March 2012. Lecture.

———. "I Want It to Be Worth It: An Interview with Emma Watson." *RookieMag*, 27 May 2013. Web. 25 Feb. 2015.

Gittens, Georgina. "Gabrielle Turnquest: The World's Youngest Barrister." *Chambers Women and Diversity*, 28 Aug. 2013. Web. 25 Jan. 2015.

"Give Hope." *Love in the Mirror*, n.d. Web. 21 May 2015.

Goldstone, Nancy Bazelon. *The Maid and the Queen: The Secret History of Joan of Arc*. New York: Viking, 2012. Print.

Guerrero-Peral, A. L. "Neurological Evaluation of the Leper King Baldwin IV of Jerusalem." *Rev Neurol*. 2009 Oct 16–31;49(8):430–3. Spanish. PMID: 19816847.

Gupta, Sanjay. "Medical Breakthroughs." *Vital Signs*. July 2014. Lecture.

Hall Kimberley, Sandra. *Duke: A Great Hawaiian*. Honolulu: Bess Press, 2004. Print.

Hamilton, Bernard. *The Leper King and His Heirs: Baldwin IV and the Crusader Kingdom of Jerusalem*. Cambridge, UK: Cambridge UP, 2000. Print.

Harness, Cheryl. *Remember the Ladies: 100 Great American Women*. New York: HarperCollins, 2001. Print.

Harris, Harry. *Pelé: His Life and Times*. New York: Welcome Rain Publishers, 2001. Print.

"HeForShe." *HeForShe*. UN Women, n.d. Web. 23 Feb. 2015.

Heinemann, Sue. *The New York Public Library Amazing Women in American History: A Book of Answers for Kids*. New York: Wiley, 1998. Print.

Herman, Emma. "Emma Watson's UN Gender Equality Campaign Is an Invitation to Men, Too." *The Guardian*. Guardian News and Media Limited, 3 Oct. 2014. Web. 25 Feb. 2015.

Hicks, Johnathan P. "Asean Johnson: The 9-Year-Old Who Captivated a Nation." *BET.com*. BET, 27 Oct. 2013. Web. 21 May 2015.

Hinton, S. E. *Some of Tim's Stories*. Norman, OK: University of Oklahoma Press, 2007. Print.

Hoose, Phillip M. *Claudette Colvin: Twice Toward Justice.* New York: Square Fish, 2011. Print.

Hui Nalu O Hawaii. *Hui Nalu O Hawaii,* n.d. Web. 21 Feb. 2015.

Hutchinson, Courtney. "Pre-Med for High Schoolers?" *ABC News.* ABC News Network, 21 June 2010. Web. 21 Feb. 2015.

Jaggi, Param. "Home." *Param Jaggi,* n.d. Web. 21 Feb. 2015.

———. "At 19, I Think I Can Change the World." *INKtalk.* March 2012. Lecture.

Jankeliowitch, Anne, and Yann Arthus-Bertrand. *Kids Who Are Changing the World: A Book from the GoodPlanet Foundation.* Naperville, IL: Source Jabberwocky, 2014. Print.

Jurie, Hwang. "Record IQ Is Just Another Talent." *The Korea Herald.* Herald Corporation, 06 Nov. 2010. Web. 22 Feb. 2015.

Keiter, Jane. "Deborah Sampson." *Education & Resources.* National Women's History Museum, n.d. Web. 22 Feb. 2015.

Keller, Helen. *How I Would Help the World.* West Chester, PA. Swedenborg Foundation, 2011. Print.

Kilby Borland, Kathryn, and Helen Ross Speicher. *Phillis Wheatley: Young Colonial Poet.* Indianapolis: Bobbs-Merrill Company, 1968. Print.

Kiphuth, Robert J., and Arthur Grahame. "Can We Swim Past Japan?" *Boys Life* July 1934: 13+. Print.

Knight, Frida. *Beethoven and the Age of Revolution.* United Kingdom. International Press, 1973. Print.

Knowlan, Robert A. "Maria Gaetana Agnesi." *A Chronicle of Mathematical People.* Robert A. Knowlan, n.d. Web. 13 Dec. 2014.

Ko, Lydia. "World Ladies Championship—JLPGA." *Welcome to the Website of Lydia Ko.* N.p., n.d. Web. 22 Feb. 2015.

Krull, Kathleen, and Greg Couch. *The Boy Who Invented TV: The Story of Philo Farnsworth.* New York: Alfred A. Knopf, 2009. Print.

Krull, Kathleen, and Kathryn Hewitt. *Lives of Extraordinary Women: Rulers, Rebels (and What the Neighbors Thought)*. San Diego: Harcourt, 2000. Print.

———. *Lives of the Athletes: Thrills, Spills (and What the Neighbors Thought)*. Orlando, FL. Harcourt Brace and Company, 1997. Print.

Lang, Heather, and Floyd Cooper. *Queen of the Track: Alice Coachman, Olympic High-jump Champion*. Honesdale, PA: Boyds Mills, 2012. Print.

Leal, Samantha. "10 Young Activists Changing the World—Mom.me." BermanBraun Interactive, 11 Nov. 2013. Web. 12 Dec. 2014.

León, Vicki. *4,000 Years of Uppity Women: Rebellious Belles, Daring Dames, and Headstrong Heroines Through the Ages*. New York: MJF, 2011. Print.

———. *Outrageous Women of the Middle Ages*. New York: Wiley, 1998. Print.

Li, Rosa. "Extra! Extra! Read All About the Newsboys Strike of 1899." New York Public Library, 25 May 2012. Web. 12 Dec. 2014.

"Lydia Ko Wins Women's Australian Open." *ABC News*. American Broadcasting Company, 22 Feb. 2015. Web. 22 Feb. 2015.

MacLeod, Elizabeth. *Helen Keller: A Determined Life*. Tonawanda, NY: Kids Can Press, 2004. Print.

Malaspina, Ann, and Eric Velasquez. *Touch the Sky: Alice Coachman, Olympic High Jumper*. Chicago: Albert Whitman, 2012. Print.

Mann, Herman. "The Female Review." *The Life of Deborah Sampson, the Female Soldier in the War of the Revolution*. Boston: J. K. Wiggin & W. P. Lunt. 1797. Print.

Marcovitz, Hal. *Modern Role Models, Venus and Serena Williams*. Broomall, PA: Mason Crest Publishers, 2009. Print.

"Maria Gaetana Agnesi." *Encyclopædia Britannica Online*. Web. 13 Dec. 2014.

Mark, Joshua J. "Kinich Janaab Pacal." *Ancient History Ency-clopedia*. Ancient History Encyclopedia Limited, 28 Mar. 2014. Web. 22 Feb. 2015.

Márquez, Marc. "Biography." *Marc Márquez 93—Official Website*. N.p., n.d. Web. 22 Feb. 2015.

"Márquez Replaces Pedrosa as Top Teenager." *Crash News*. Crash Media Group, 22 Aug. 2012. Web. 22 Feb. 2015.

"Márquez: Youngest Ever MotoGP™ Leader." *Motogp.com*., 8 May 2013. Web. 22 Feb. 2015.

Martin, Claire. "Xiuhtezcatl Roske-Martinez, 14, Wants to Save the World." *The Denver Post*. MediaNewsGroup, 25 May 2014. Web. 21 May 2015.

Martinez, Xiuhtezcatl. *Earth Guardians*. N.p., n.d. Web. 21 May 2015.

Max, D. T. "The Prince's Gambit." *The New Yorker*. Advance Publications, 21 Mar. 2011. Web. 24 Jan. 2015.

McCann, Michelle Roehm, and Amelie Welden. *Girls Who Rocked the World: Heroines from Joan of Arc to Mother Teresa*. New York: Aladdin, 2012. Print.

Mellor, C. Michael. *Louis Braille: A Touch of Genius*. Boston: National Braille, 2006. Print.

Mesoweb, Jorge Pérez de Lara, Mark Van Stone, Merle Greene Robertson, Joel Skidmore, et al. "K'inich Janaab Pakal I." *Mesoweb Encyclopedia*. N.p., n.d. Web. 22 Feb. 2015.

Meyers, Jessica. "Young Inventor's Algae Device May One Day Revolutionize Air Quality." *The Dallas Morning News*. DMN Media, 18 Sept. 2011. Web. 21 Feb. 2015.

Mock, Brentin. "Tony Hansberry, Whiz-Kid Considered 'the Next Charles Drew.'" *The Grio*, 03 Feb. 2010. Web. 21 Feb. 2015.

National Braille Press. N.d. Web. 27 Dec. 2014.

National Federation of the Blind. N.d. Web. 27 Dec. 2014.

Newman, Brad. "Rosie Casals, Tennis' Salvadoran Spitfire." *Hispanic Heritage Month. Fox News Latino*. 8 Sept. 2012. Fox News Latino. Web. 2 Jan. 2015.

Novas, Himilce. *The Hispanic 100: A Ranking of the Latino Men and Women Who Have Most Influenced American Thought and Culture.* New York: Citadel Press, 1995. Print.

Ogilvie, Marilyn Bailey. *Women in Science: Antiquity Through the Nineteenth Century: A Biographical Dictionary with Annotated Bibliography.* Cambridge, MA: MIT, 1986. Print.

Osen, Lynn M. *Women in Mathematics.* Cambridge, MA: MIT, 1974. Print.

Pearl, Diana. "Ballerina Misty Copeland Urges Young Women to 'Stay Strong,' Plus Advice from Chelsea Clinton, Ivanka Trump and More." *People Magazine,* 21 Sept. 2015. Web. 25 Sept. 2015.

Pelé, and Fish, Robert L. *My Life and the Beautiful Game: The Autobiography of Pelé.* New York: Skyhorse Publishing, 1977. Print.

Perez, Chris. *To Selena, with Love.* New York: Celebra, 2012. Print.

Polland, Jennifer. "This Nanoparticle System May Lead to a Cure for Cancer." *Business Insider,* 10 Aug. 2012. Web. 17 Feb. 2015.

Rave Lee, Jodi. "New Story of Sacagawea." *Rapid City Journal Online.* N.d. Web. 17 Feb. 2015.

Richens, Matt. "Newly-Crowned World No 1 Ko 'Miffed' She Didn't Win." *Stuff.* Fairfax Media, 1 Feb. 2015. Web. 22 Feb. 2015.

Rolka, Gail Meyer. *100 Women Who Shaped World History.* San Francisco: Bluewood, 1994. Print.

Rountree, Helen, and Camilla Townsend. "Jamestown: What Pocahontas Saw." Podcast. *With Good Reason.* Virginia Foundation for the Humanities, 14 Jan. 2006. Web. 29 Dec. 2014.

Rountree, Helen C. *Pocahontas, Powhatan, Opechancanough: Three Indian Lives Changed by Jamestown.* Charlottesville: U of Virginia, 2006. Print.

Schaller, K. B. *100+ Native American Women Who Changed the World.*: Peppertree Press, 2013. Print.

Schwartz, Evan I. *Philo T. Farnsworth vs David Barnoff in the Last Lone Inventor: A Tale of Genius, Deceit, and the Birth of Television.* New York: HarperCollins, 2002. Print.

"Selena Quintanilla Perez Tribute." *SelenaForever.com.* N.p., n.d. Web. 25 Feb. 2015.

Shecter, Vicky Alvear. *Alexander the Great Rocks the World.* Plain City, OH: Darby Creek Pub., 2006. Print.

Shelley, Mary Wollstonecraft. *Frankenstein; Or, the Modern Prometheus.* London: Lackington, Hughes, Harding, Mavor & Jones, 1818. Print.

Sitaraman, Nicole Williams, and Judy Chaikin. "Melba Liston." *The Girls in the Band.* One Step Productions, n.d. Documentary. May 2013.

"Smith, Powhatan, & Pocahontas." *Captain John Smith Chesapeake Historic Trail.* National Park Services, n.d. Web. 28 Dec. 2014.

Spoto, Donald. *Joan: The Mysterious Life of the Heretic Who Became a Saint.* New York: HarperSanFrancisco, 2007. Print.

St. George, Judith. *Sacagawea.* New York: G. P. Putnam's Sons, 1997. Print.

Stashower, Daniel. *The Boy Genius and the Mogul: The Untold Story of Television.* New York: Broadway, 2002. Print.

Taibbi, Matt. "Teenage Cycling Prodigy Leads Afghan Women to New Freedoms." *NBC News.* NBC, 28 Mar. 2013. Web. 21 Feb. 2015.

Thimmesh, Catherine, and Melissa Sweet. *Girls Think of Everything: Stories of Ingenious Inventions by Women.* Boston: Houghton Mifflin, 2000. Print.

Townes, Carimah. "Emma Watson Becomes United Nations Ambassador, Will Encourage Men to Speak Up for Women." *ThinkProgress.* 08 July 2014. Web. 25 Feb. 2015.

Turnquest, Gabrielle. "I promise I'm not just collecting degrees." Twitter, 2014. Web.

Venkatraman, Padma. *Women Mathematicians.* Greensboro, NC: Morgan Reynolds Pub., 2009. Print.

Watson, Emma. "Gender Equality Is Your Issue Too." *UN Women*, 20 Sept. 2014. Speech.

Williams, Tenley. *Stevie Wonder: Overcoming Adversity.* Philadelphia: Chelsea House Publishers, 2002. Print.

Williamson, Allen. "Primary Sources and Context Concerning Joan of Arc's Male Clothing." *Historical Academy (Association) for Joan of Arc Studies.* 2006. PDF.

Wilson, Matt. "Monta Vista Grad Angela Zhang Continues Success at Harvard after Winning Siemens Competition." *San Jose Mercury News.* 18 Dec. 2013. Web. 17 Feb. 2015.

Woodlief, Anne. "Wheatley Biography." Virginia Commonwealth University, n.d. Web. 23 Feb. 2015.

Young, Alfred Fabian. *Masquerade: The Life and Times of Deborah Sampson, Continental Soldier.* New York: Vintage, 2005. Print.

Zapruder, Alexandra. *Anne Frank.* Washington, D.C.: National Geographic Society, 2013. Print.

Zhang, Angela. "Breaking Down the Unknown." *TEDxTeen.* April 2012. Lecture.

Recommended Reading

Abdul-Jabbar, Kareem, Raymond Obstfeld, Ben Boos, and A. G. Ford. *What Color Is My World?: The Lost History of African-American Inventors*. Somerville, MA: Candlewick, 2012. Print.

Beaton, Kate. "Hark!: A Vagrant." Montréal: *Drawn & Quarterly*, 2011. Print.

Chin-Lee, Cynthia, Megan Halsey, and Sean Addy. *Amelia to Zora: Twenty-Six Women Who Changed the World*. Watertown, MA: Charlesbridge, 2005. Print.

Harness, Cheryl. *Remember the Ladies: 100 Great American Women*. New York: HarperCollins, 2001. Print.

Heinemann, Sue. *The New York Public Library Amazing Women in American History: A Book of Answers for Kids*. New York: Wiley, 1998. Print.

León, Vicki. *Outrageous Women of the Middle Ages*. New York: Wiley, 1998. Print.

McCann, Michelle Roehm. *Boys Who Rocked the World: Heroes from King Tut to Bruce Lee*. New York: Aladdin, 2012. Print.

McCann, Michelle Roehm, and Amelie Welden. *Girls Who Rocked the World: Heroines from Joan of Arc to Mother Teresa*. New York: Aladdin, 2012. Print.

Stabler, David. *Kid Athletes: True Tales of Childhood from Sports Legends*. Philadelphia: Quirk Books, 2015. Print.

Thimmesh, Catherine, and Melissa Sweet. *Girls Think of Everything: Stories of Ingenious Inventions by Women*. Boston: Houghton Mifflin, 2000. Print.

Wulffson, Don L. *The Kid Who Invented the Popsicle: And Other Surprising Stories About Inventions*. New York: Puffin, 1999. Print.

Acknowledgments

My many thanks to my daughter Gwen, for being an expert bibliographer; to my husband Jason, for being an expert librarian; to my HLM Wendi, for additional research assistance and all the musical inspiration a girl almighty could hope for. The biggest of thanks to my editor, Dana Bergman, who is unfailingly thoughtful, thorough, and enthusiastic—and to my agent, Jim McCarthy, whose support never wavers.   —SM

I am ever grateful to my husband, Steve, who is the best studio assistant/life partner a gal could hope for. Thanks for always making dinner and scanning sketches and line art.

My agent, Nancy Moore, is nothing but the steadfast best. The lady works hard, has my back, and believes in me. Eileen Kreit, Dana Bergman, Irene Vandervoort, and the entire Puffin team, you are wonderful to collaborate with and I blush at your compliments—thank you.

Finally, Saundra Mitchell, thanks for writing smart books for smart kids. Also, you gave me the opportunity to draw portrait after portrait, and few things are better in a day in this illustrator's life— thank you.   —CP